Handbook for Technical Writing

Handbook for Technical Writing

James H. Shelton III

Printed on recyclable paper

NTC Business Books
a division of *NTC Publishing Group* • Lincolnwood, Illinois USA

Library of Congress Cataloging-in-Publication Data

Shelton, James H.
Handbook For technical writing/James H. Shelton.
p. cm.
ISBN 0-8442-3275-0 (hard). — ISBN 0-8442-3276-9 (pbk.)
1. English language–Technical English–Handbooks, manual, etc. 2. English language–Rhetoric–Handbooks, manuals, etc. 3. Technical writing–Handbooks, manuals, etc. I. Title.
PE1475.S48 1994
808'.0666–dc20 93-17444
CIP

1996 Printing

Published by NTC Business Books, a division of NTC Publishing Group.

Manufactured in the United States of America.

6 7 8 9 0 VP 9 8 7 6 5 4

CONTENTS

Section 1
THE STYLE OF TECHNICAL WRITING

Section 2
THE PROCESS OF TECHNICAL WRITING: Six Steps For Success

Section 3
THE ELEMENTS OF TECHNICAL WRITING

Section 4
FORMS OF TECHNICAL WRITING I:
Memo Reports and Formal Reports

Section 5
FORMS OF TECHNICAL WRITING II: Proposals, Manuals, and Journal Articles

Appendix
THE MECHANICS OF TECHNICAL WRITING

Section 1

THE STYLE OF TECHNICAL WRITING

1.1 What Is Technical Writing?

Technical writing communicates specific and factual information to a defined audience for a defined purpose. The information is technical in nature, and this is what makes technical writing different from other types of writing. Broadly, that audience includes technical readers, managerial readers, or even, at times, general readers. The purpose is to inform, instruct, describe, explain, or otherwise document scientific or industrial processes and mechanisms.

You will readily discover some overlap between technical writing and business writing, but the two have many distinct differences, both in terms of subject matter and document format. Whereas commerce and the business community govern the subject matter of business writing, technical writing deals primarily with the hard sciences and the industrial community. The primary documents of business writing are letters, memorandas, and business reports. The primary documents of technical writing are technical reports, manuals, and instructions.

Despite their differences, business and technical writing share the same principles of good writing. Both are concerned with delivering factual information in a clear, concise, and objective manner.

Technical writing has actually been around for all of recorded history. Leonardo da Vinci certainly was writing technical documents when he made notes on his drawings of mechanical wings. Certainly the writings of Newton, Copernicus, and Hippocrates could also be considered technical writing.

However, for many centuries the writings of these great thinkers were confined to the intellectual elite at great universities, whereas ordinary men and women performed manual labor, using tools that required little or no explanation. Eventually, as literacy and the use of more complex tools and machinery spread during the Industrial Revolution, the need for explanations of mechanical processes grew rapidly.

The discipline of modern technical writing came of age during World War II. Increasingly sophisticated technical processes were used to manufacture weapons, culminating with the invention of nuclear bombs. Communications developments during this time allowed the spread of technical documents more than ever before.

The next great surge came with the computer revolution. Since the development of the first powerful mainframes in the 1960s, instruction, description, and documentation within the high-tech arena have become crucial to every facet of our work and home lives. Today, everything from automobile owner's manuals describing computerized dashboards to the instructions for booting up personal computers floods us with technical information.

1.1.1 Who Writes Technical Documents?

There are professional technical writers who do nothing but write. Some of them work within industry to develop users manuals, scripts for training films, or marketing material for industrial equipment. Others work as freelancers on individual projects within their areas of technical expertise. There are also professionals such as engineers, scientists, and technicians who do various types of technical writing as a necessary part of their everyday work. They write memoranda to inform their supervisors of progress, journal articles to contribute to the collective knowledge of their disciplines, and grant proposals for government support. Most technical writing is done by these technical professionals. Students make up another large group whose success depends on clear, concise, accurate writing.

1.1.2 The Need for Clear and Concise Technical Writing

Never has there been a greater need for clear and concise technical writing. The more scientifically complex our world becomes, the greater the need for direct, simple, and clear communication. World knowledge currently doubles about every year. Many of these data are documented in one form or another. Manuals, texts, field reports, instructions, and progress reports create a mind-boggling amount of information. Scientists, engineers, and technicians need clear communication to understand one another's work and the rapid changes taking place in their fields of expertise. Managers and marketers in technology-driven industries need clear and concise information to help them communicate successfully beyond their own technical areas. Systems engineers need clear writing to design local area networks to link personal computers and software that runs on them. In all of these cases, the ability to communicate clearly and concisely is key. Though the subject matter is, by definition, complicated, technical writing must *not* be. Technical writing must help, not hinder, the communication of complex ideas.

Technical writing that succeeds conveys a message that is accurate, useful, and objective. As a primary goal, it transmits to the reader factual information that is crystal clear. Technical writing always concentrates on content, rather than style. A technical writer must sacrifice the ego of personal writing style for the sake of clear technical content. The technical message is paramount in all cases.

The dangers of unclear technical messages cannot be overstated. An auto mechanic who misinterprets instructions for rebuilding brakes can be the unwilling cause of tragedy. Line engineers in an assembly plant likewise depend on clear technical writing to manufacture dependable, high-quality products. Hospital patients rely on medical technicians' ability to comprehend support documentation for diagnostic equipment.

1.2 Readers Get First Consideration

In technical writing, your readers should always come first. Although it's tempting to first consider content, approach, and style, don't do this at the expense of clarity. Your purpose is to inform—make sure you write to your readers' level of understanding.

Readers dictate the success of any piece of writing. It doesn't matter how well *you* understand the subject matter if *your readers* miss the message. If they don't understand, your writing has failed. Think first of your audience. Evaluate their needs as well as their ability to understand technical content.

We can class the readers of technical documents into three broad categories: *technical readers*, *managerial readers*, and *general readers*. Let's consider them in terms of their needs and their level of understanding.

1.2.1 Technical Readers

Technical readers are different from managerial and general readers. Technical readers have deep knowledge about the content of your particular written communication. This knowledge may be a general knowledge of the subject or it may be detailed knowledge. In either case, to fit in this category, readers must *technically know* your subject. Be especially careful to allow them to get directly to the idea without fighting your writing.

Superficial verbosity meant either to impress them or to accommodate their technical knowledge will fail. Do not ever assume that because they have advanced technical knowledge and understanding, they prefer writing loaded with long sentences and unnecessary words. Once again, technical readers prefer a direct and simplified written approach. This allows them to deal with difficult concepts instead of difficult writing.

Technical readers fall into two groups: *theorists* and *technicians*. The two groups overlap, but they have basic differences in their approach to technical subjects.

Theorists

Any technical person involved in pure research is a theorist. This highly theoretical concern translates into such areas as scientific research and design theory. The astronomer who strives to validate the existence of black holes and to explain the nature of quasars is a technical theorist. The chemist who works to synthesize a new and stronger plastic and the doctor on a research team looking for new ways to open partially blocked coronary arteries are both theorists.

Writing directed to this group is generally the most difficult to read. Somehow the notion prevails that easily understood writing is somehow insulting to theorists. This notion may have evolved from a preoccupation with academic writing, which can sometimes be difficult to read and understand. This notion carries over to real-world research papers and articles on new discoveries. In fact, theorists don't want to read difficult writing. Highly theoretical writing need not be difficult and boring. The theory may be complex and difficult, but the writing can be clear and concise.

Technicians

Technicians are primarily concerned with the practical aspects of technology. They repair, maintain, and operate mechanisms and control processes. Electricians, nurses, and hydraulics mechanics are all technicians.

Forms of writing commonly directed to this group are technical manuals, mechanical descriptions, and various types of documentation required in a technical workplace. Because technicians solve the day-to-day problems of science and industry, they must understand what they read as quickly and easily as possible.

1.2.2 Managerial Readers

Managerial readers need to be informed, yet they often do not need the technical detail and depth that theorists and technicians need. Remember that the title of "manager" indicates job responsibility rather than technical knowledge. The managerial reader might not have the technical understanding of the purely technical reader. This is why the "Executive Summary" has become a common and valuable tool in technical report writing. The executive summary reduces an entire technical document to the plain facts a manager needs to make decisions. The report itself will contain technical details a managerial reader may not fully comprehend. Therefore, the executive summary must accurately describe the key points of information in nontechnical language.

Managerial readers come from various technical backgrounds, however. The Director of Research and Development is most likely both manager and expert. The Engineering Manager is also probably both expert and manager. The Director of Admissions at a teaching and research hospital may be primarily a manager. The Maintenance Manager of a large spread of construction equipment is more than likely a manager *and* a technician.

To succeed with this group, you must get straight to the point. Managers generally are flooded with written information and do not have time to read rambling, unclear prose. Concise writing is key with a managerial audience.

1.2.3 General Readers

General readers usually have the least technical knowledge and understanding of your particular subject. Consequently, you must write clearly and concisely for this group while addressing their level of technical understanding. This does not mean you should write down to them. This type of reader will have enough challenge understanding your concepts without struggling with your writing. General readers are a vital audience for technical business and industry—they are the customers!

Generally readers do not necessarily lack technical knowledge and understanding. A surgeon who just bought a personal computer may be a neophyte where the product is concerned, yet a technical reader in the field of medicine. The issue, once again, is the need for simplified, direct, understandable language.

1.3 Expressing versus Impressing

Many professionals who write about technical subjects face the dilemma of whether to impress readers or to express ideas that convey information. It may seem obvious that expressing ideas and conveying information is the right way to approach technical writing, yet the urge to impress readers is all too prevalent.

Consider this classic example of writing that struggles with expressing rather than impressing. A plumber had used hydrochloric acid to clear some clogged pipes. The process worked quickly and cleared the drain. The plumber then wrote to a government research organization in Washington, D.C., to tell them of the expedient method and ask for their appraisal. The agency wrote back as follows:

> The efficacy of hydrochloric acid is indisputable, but the highly corrosive residue is incompatible with metallic permanence.

Highly encouraged, the plumber wrote back that he was glad they agreed with this use of the acid. Concerned about the apparent failure in communication, a different member of the agency wrote back as follows:

> We cannot assume direct or indirect responsibility for the possible production of toxic and highly noxious residue obtained from the hydrochloric acid and ascertain that you should examine alternative procedures.

Encouraged by the second letter and the apparent enthusiasm of the agency, the plumber wrote back that the acid was working great and that they should recommend its universal use in freeing clogged plumbing. Disturbed over this turn of events, a third member of the agency wrote back this time saying:

> Don't use hydrochloric acid. It eats the hell out of pipes.

The problem here was not with the plumber. The problem was with the first two writers, whose words took on the attitude and image of the scientific agency where they were employed. They needed to "look" and "sound" professional. The result was writing that was needlessly obscured, pompous, and self-important. The primary motive in the first two answers the plumber received was to *impress*. The third answer was written to *express* at the most expedient level.

It is quite natural for professionals to want a professional image. When it comes to writing, clear, concise, and simple messages have the greatest impact on image. Long, wordy, pompous writing neither expresses nor impresses.

1.4 The Academic Influence

A major contributing factor to obscure and difficult technical writing is the nature of academic writing. Try as they may, our university classrooms do not approximate the real workplace. Usually students do not *know* but rather are *learning* the material they are writing about. The prime mission of an academic paper often is to impress the instructor with what the student has learned. A good instructor does not and should not take for granted that the student knows the subject area. Because of the nature of the academic experience, everything becomes an exercise to demonstrate learning.

Upon entering the professional world, the entire writing emphasis changes. Now your professional knowledge is taken for granted—after all, you have been hired in a professional capacity. Your writing now focuses on the transfer of information and ideas. This transfer of information is not an exercise in impressing readers but rather an action that expresses thoughts in clear, concise language. You must make your written messages as clear and understandable as possible.

1.5 Clarity

There are two major elements in achieving clarity in your writing: a preference for shorter sentences and the use of active language. These elements assure clear and understandable technical writing.

1.5.1 Shorter Sentences

In technical writing, there is probably no greater problem than needlessly long sentences. The more words there are to read in a sentence, the more you must keep track of and understand. A compound, complex, or compound-complex sentence is always harder to read and understand than a simple declarative sentence. When a technical report, manual, or set of instructions is loaded with these long and complex sentences, the difficulty increases. Never allow sentences to become any more complicated than is absolutely necessary. Sentences are like baggage. Only carry what you need and not a bit more.

A common misconception is that highly educated people *prefer* longer and more complicated writing. You would be mistaken ever to believe that because your readers have a highly technical background, they will prefer longer sentences. They do not.

Long sentences make your reader try to keep track of more information than is easily managed. It is not that the mind cannot do it but rather that your reader tires of constantly doing it. A single long sentence at intervals throughout the writing does not pose the reader a problem. It is when every sentence is long and difficult that the reader tires and begins to lose interest and drive. As sentences approach 20–30 words, it becomes difficult to keep straight all the information in them. When a sentence goes beyond 30 words, it becomes all but impossible to read without going back and studying it for meaning. The following sentence is too long and needs revision:

> It certainly appears that once the tests have been finalized on the new polymer for the motor housings, we can gain a firm and clear consensus on what actions concerning the replacement or the continuance of present housing materials should be, because the next run on housing is due on the 15th of next month. [55 words]

After being revised, it consists of two sentences of 21 words and 20 words:

> After testing the new polymer for motor housings, we must make a final decision on whether to use it or not. We must decide on which polymer to use before the next production run, scheduled for the 15th of next month.

1.5.2 Active Language

Action coupled with a direct statement is at the heart of effective technical writing. Strong, active verbs give your writing energy and power that add interest and understanding to the message. Weak, passive verbs rob your writing of power and interest. Your use of verbs in technical writing controls meaning and understanding.

Verbs express either action or state of being. Action verbs convey movement and energy. They promote a vigorous style of prose that *shows* readers the message rather than just *telling them about it*. State-of-being verbs are all forms of the verb *to be*. Such words as *is, are, am, was, were, been,* and *being* are some forms of this verb.

Action verbs can describe events in either an *active voice* or a *passive voice*. In the active voice, the subject of the sentence names the entity that performed the action. In the passive voice, the subject names the entity that was acted upon. Sentences in the active voice have a direct subject-verb-object structure. Sentences in the passive voice have an indirect structure: the object, a helping form of the verb *to be*, and the past participle of the action verb. The subject of a passive sentence is either implied or introduced indirectly with a prepositional phrase. The way in which you use these two voices is crucial to how clearly and directly the meaning will come across to your reader.

Both the active voice and the passive voice have their distinct advantages. The problem of active versus passive lies in the *frequent abuse of the passive voice* in technical writing. Unfortunately, many persons in the technical, scientific, and industrial communities suppress forceful and active writing because of an unwarranted demand for impersonal language. Consider the following sentences written in the passive voice:

1. All Engineering Change Notices must be approved by the engineering manager.
2. Antiseptic content was not properly analyzed by our satellite lab.
3. Excessive engine wear is also characterized by low compression readings.
4. The faulty valve was quickly found by the emergency maintenance crew.
5. The voltage across the circuit was measured by assembly personnel at three different points.

In each sentence, the passive voice places the receiver of the action as the subject. The doer of the action is in a subordinate position at the end of the sentence. Now consider each of the previous sentences rewritten in the active voice:

1. The engineering manager must approve all Engineering Change Notices.
2. Our satellite lab improperly analyzed antiseptic content.
3. Low compression readings also characterize excessive engine wear.
4. The emergency maintenance crew quickly found the faulty valve.
5. Assembly personnel measured the voltage across the circuit at three different points.

Each sentence now has the doer of the action as its subject. In each case, the doer is at least as important as the receiver of the action.

Changing verb constructions to the active voice helps each sentence in two ways. First, each thought becomes a logical route from cause to effect (doer to receiver). Second, the writer uses fewer words when using the active voice. You don't need helping verbs with past participles, and you don't need prepositional phrases to introduce the doer of the action. Remember that economy of words is the essence of concise and direct writing.

At this point a word of caution is in order. You should not summarily dismiss the passive voice from the English language. On the contrary, the passive voice does have a place in good technical prose. The passive voice is an effective tool of communication when the doer of the action is not important to the reader. In such cases the passive voice is preferred. Consider the following two sentences:

Active Voice: In May, Acme Heating Company will install new electronic air cleaners in both clean rooms.

Passive Voice: In May, new electronic air cleaners will be installed in both clean rooms.

Acme Heating, the installer of the electronic air cleaners, is not important to the message. The reader does not really care who installs the electronic air cleaners. The emphasis is on the new air cleaners and their date of installation. Consequently, the use of the passive voice in this case emphasizes the electronic air cleaners (receivers of the action) and does not even mention Acme Heating (the doers of the action).

Remember, however, that *preference for the active voice* is the keystone to direct and forcible writing. A lifeless and boring passage can often be revived simply by using the active voice.

1.5.3 Suppressed Verbs

Turning a verb into a noun suppresses the verb's ability to act. Frequently, active verbs are turned into nouns and used with state-of-being verb forms. These verbs become an event rather than an action. This forced passivity stifles direct and active writing. Take notice of noun endings such as *-tion*, *-ance*, *-ment*, *ing*, *-al*, and *-ancy*. These will often signal a suppressed verb.

Suppressed verb constructions are underlined in the examples below. Each is an action expressed as an event. Notice how these constructions add hollow wordiness to the sentences. When suppressed verbs are rewritten into activated verbs, sentences gain action and force.

Suppressed Verbs

1. Performance of the new stabilizer was far better than past designs.
2. Stabilization of the compound took place early in the experiment.
3. The milling of the three steel bases was done in the new computerized machining center.
4. Performance of the turbines was not acceptable by industry standards.
5. Evaporation of the fuel will take place in a matter of seconds.

Suppressed Verbs Rewritten as Activated Verbs

1. The new stabilizer performed far better than past designs.
2. The compound stabilized early in the experiment.
3. The three steel bases were milled in the new computerized machining center.
4. The turbines performed unacceptably by industry standards.
5. The fuel will evaporate in a matter of seconds.

Once again, a small change in verb structure brought about a large improvement toward direct, active writing.

1.5.4 Needless Verbs

Technical writers often add needless verb constructions to a sentence. These constructions add to the sentence's complexity and difficulty without adding meaning. This results in writing that seeks to impress rather than express. In the following sentences, the underlined verbs are needless.

1. Alignment of the cutting tool on the arbor must be accomplished by using spacers.
2. Caloric oxidation is dependent on regular exercise for burning.
3. The analysis of the anti-rust coating shows a large variation from earlier tests.
4. Rubber is strengthened by using sulphur and other additives.
5. You must examine the earlier test results that were involved.

Activate these sentences by eliminating each needless verb:

1. Use spacers to align the cutting tool on the arbor.

2. Regular exercise burns calories.
3. Analysis of the anti-rust coating varies greatly from earlier tests.
4. Sulphur and other additives strengthen rubber.
5. You must examine the earlier test results.

1.5.5 Personal versus Impersonal Constructions

There is much debate about whether technical writing must be strictly impersonal or whether it should use personal references. The trend is unmistakably moving toward the use of active personal references. This trend promotes the use of the active voice. Professional journals have used the first- and second-person pronouns for a number of years now.

Nevertheless, many organizations forbid the use of personal direct reference in their publications. In its place, writers continue to twist and torture technical writing with tangled and passive constructions. The professional journals, along with the consumer press, discovered long ago that people don't read boring, impersonal abstractions. Must formal technical reports and the like remain bogged down in impersonal, obscure, passive writing? The answer is found in the changes that have begun to take place among organizations that are striving to retrain their staffs in the art and craft of clear and active technical writing. Modern technical writing respects a reader's need to know the doer of the action. Consider the following sentences:

1. It has been requested that the samples taken at five different points on the river be retested for PCBs.
2. Limitations must be imposed on the scope of this project.
3. It is necessary that a water-base coolant be used.

The first sentence contains the "It ... that" construction, probably one of the most overworked constructions in technical writing. In almost every such case, you can strengthen and shorten the sentence by employing the active voice.

1. Management has asked us to retest the samples we had taken at five different points on the river.
2. You must limit the scope of this project.
3. Use a water-base coolant.

1.5.6 Making Verbs from Adjectives and Nouns

Language purists sometimes forget that language is dynamic. With the onslaught of the high-tech industries and their particular jargons, use of adjectives and nouns as verbs has become quite common. When abused, this approach to language becomes elitist. When not overdone, this approach can be a useful tool for direct and meaningful communication. Consider the following nouns and adjectives used as verbs:

Nouns	**Adjectives**
position	final
service	formal
immunity	local

Verbs

... to position the stylus.
... to service the compressor.
... to immunize only the primary grades.
... to finalize the stress tests.
... to formalize the procedures.
... to localize the anesthetic.

1.6 When to Use the Past and Present Tense

Debate sometimes arises over whether to use the present or past tense in a technical report. The general approach is to describe completed action in the past tense. Describe principles, instructions, and conclusions in the present tense. Consider the following sentences:

1. Five of the tests showed weak patterns. [completed action]
2. These high-compression readings show negligible ring wear. [conclusion]
3. Set the timer for 15 seconds. [instructions]
4. The Doppler effect shows a red color shift for stars moving away from our position in the galaxy. [principle]

1.7 Conciseness

Concise writing provides exactly what the reader needs and not a bit more or less. Bloated writing with superfluous information serves to confuse and obscure. Concise writing gets to the point and does not ramble. There is nothing that will kill a reader's interest faster than rambling, affected writing that takes five pages to say what could be said in one paragraph.

1.7.1 Brevity

Brevity is at the heart of getting to the point. You must use an economy of words that allows the reader to get the message immediately.

There is the story of a person who when asked the time of day gave a short history of Swiss watchmaking before telling what time it was. Don't do this to your reader. Get to the point in the shortest route that still allows the reader to understand. In the following sentence, what should be a direct and concise statement rambles:

> A decision on this matter must be made in a prompt manner before the deadline comes and goes.

This sentence can be fixed simply by stating only what is needed in the active voice:

> We must decide on this before the deadline.

1.7.2 Redundancy and Clichés

To be concise demands one-time statements that are clear and need no repetition. Redundancy occurs when statements are repeated needlessly. This needless repetition comes in the form of affected writing and clichés. In technical writing, make precise statements that speak to the reader only once. In the following examples, note the redundancy and how it has been eliminated:

> A decision was made to stop the project.

When you or someone "makes a decision," you or someone "decides." A better sentence without the wordiness might be:

> We decided to stop the project.

Clichés can also cause redundancy in technical writing:

> At this point in time, the motor housings will remain square in shape.

All references to time refer to some "point in time." Anything that is square is "square in shape." These clichés create redundancy. A better sentence would be as follows:

At this time, the motor housing will remain square.

Some clichés to avoid are as follows:

• at this point in time —	at this time
• during the course of —	during
• in the vast majority of cases —	in most cases
• on a weekly basis —	weekly
• until such time as —	until
• due to the fact that —	due to
• very necessary —	necessary
• few in number —	few
• square in shape —	square

1.7.3 Affected and Vague Words

A technical vocabulary is absolutely necessary for accurate technical communication. Words in a technical vocabulary are necessary even though they may be long and hard to read. There is no other way to refer to an isotope or an oscilloscope other than to use those terms. The challenge lies in keeping the rest of your word usage simple. You should use common words where possible and use difficult technical terms only where they are needed.

For example, the following words are some fairly common technical terms used in the field of hydraulics:

- fittings
- solenoid valve
- tandem-center spool
- fixed-displacement double-vane pump
- venting

All of these words are needed within the context of a technical piece of writing in the field of industrial hydraulics. They are precise terms with precise technical meanings. You must use these terms within the context of hydraulics because there are no easier or commonly known substitutes. Pronouns will not substitute either, because pronouns must first have an antecedent—the term itself.

The problem lies less often with difficult technical terms than with an affectation of vocabulary. Affected nontechnical words can be replaced by simpler, common words. Consider the following examples:

- ascertain— find out
- contiguous— touching
- elucidate— make clear
- expedite— hurry along
- facile— easy
- periphery— outer edge
- subsequently— later
- tenuous— thin
- tortuous— twisting
- utilize— use

In each case, a word has been replaced with a far more familiar word. By using the more commonplace word, you make it easier for your reader.

1.7.4 The Concrete Use of Language

In technical writing (as opposed to literature), adverbs and adjectives do not describe their verbs and nouns exactly and concretely.

How heavy is *very heavy*? How acute is *quite acute*? In technical writing, you must write with exact and concrete terms and concepts. In the following example, vague and abstract use of language has been converted to concrete and exact use of language:

> The roadbed must be made with added strength and durability. [vague]
>
> The roadbed must be paved over reinforcement-bar (rebar) for added strength and durability. [exact and concrete]

The roadbed in the first sentence is "made," as opposed to the specific "paved over with reinforcement-bar (rebar)" in the second sentence. The words "strength" and "durability" are vague in the context of the first sentence because they have no specific and concrete reference. In the second sentence, they are defined and made specific with reference to reinforcement-bar.

1.7.5 Gobbledygook

Gobbledygook is a particular fondness for buzzwords, redundancy, and overstatement. It is pure affectation. Many people mistakenly think that this overstatement and affected usage make the writing sound official and scientific. They also think that it is indicative of an educated and adept writer. In actuality, gobbledygook signals poor writing and an inability to express yourself. The example that follows is typical gobbledygook. Notice how it has been simplified and made concise for the reader.

> ***Gobbledygook:*** In the event of life-threatening conflagration, expeditiously transport your person through the indicated egress of closest proximity to your location.
>
> ***Translation:*** In case of fire, quickly leave through the nearest door marked "EXIT."

The challenge of technical writing is to present complicated ideas with the goal of expressing, not impressing. When the technical writer abandons consideration of personal style and concentrates on delivering factual information clearly, concisely, and objectively, the technical audience benefits. Technical writers achieve this goal by understanding their audience. They strive for short, active sentences and eliminate redundancy, clichés, and gobbledygook. They prefer personal constructions and concrete language.

Writer's Workshop

1 Examine a recent technical document from your field of expertise. It can be either something you have written or something a colleague has written. Compare the style of the writing with:

(a) a popular novel;
(b) a movie or gossip magazine;
(c) a piece of poetry;
(d) a newspaper editorial page;
(e) copy from a magazine ad.

How does each of the above compare with the style of the technical writing document? What are the major differences? Similarities?

2 You are writing about the inherent problems of converting from gasoline-powered cars to electrical-powered cars. How would your writing differ, if it was targeted to the following types of readers:

(a) technical readers;
(b) managerial readers;
(c) general readers.

How are the styles different and in what specific ways? How are they similar and in what ways?

3 List the various characteristics that signal writing meant to *impress* rather than *express*. If possible, show examples of writing you have that can demonstrate these points.

4 Study a recent technical document in your field of expertise and consider the following:

(a) the variation in sentence length, throughout;
(b) the number of active versus passive sentence constructions;
(c) personal versus impersonal tone.

Rewrite the document using shorter sentences, more active-voice constructions, and a more personal tone.

5 Without referring to the lists in the text, prepare your own list of:
   (a) clichés;
   (b) affected words;
   (c) most needed technical terms you use in your field of expertise.

Self-Test Quiz

1 Technical writing is meant to be understood only by highly educated scientists, engineers, and technicians.

2 Concise writing gives only needed information to the reader.

3 Clear writing avoids intricate detail because of its tendency to confuse or be misunderstood.

4 Highly complex subjects call for a highly complex approach to writing.

5 Scientists and technicians do not require the definitions of terms and concepts that a non-technical reader requires.

6 Managerial readers may or may not be technical readers also.

7 General readers are the easiest audience for whom to write.

8 Personal tone in technical writing promotes the active voice and adds clarity to the message.

9 The active voice is preferred over the passive voice.

10 In highly technical documents, longer sentences are preferred to shorter sentences.

Answer Key

1 F **2** T **3** F **4** F **5** T **6** T **7** F **8** T **9** T **10** F

Section 2

The Process of Technical Writing: Six Steps for Success

Good technical writing takes discipline and strict adherence to a system. Much like technical knowledge and skill, writing follows an orderly sequence of events that lead to clear and concise technical prose. Whether you are designing circuits or writing instructions for a new computer program, technical writing is systematically structuring technical ideas on paper.

As you use and master this process, keep in mind that it will vary in intricacy, and at times its separate parts will overlap. There is quite a difference between a complete operations manual and a brief technical memo. In the memo, you may only have to list the points that you need to make. On the other hand, the process may become extensive for the manual.

Remember that this system is geared to help you get the job done. You will certainly find variations in the way that you put the system to work for you, but the basic system will remain in place. Make no mistake: writing is hard work. Getting started is hard. Staying with the writing to its completion is hard. This process will help you with your technical writing in much the same way that a map helps you get to your destination in the most direct and effective manner.

2.1 Think and Prepare Before You Write

This may seem too obvious to mention. It is not. The average technical professional who is behind on a writing deadline does just the opposite of this sage advice.

You live in an internationally competitive environment that demands action now. Technical reports, memos, and manuals do not escape this commercial pressure. You do not have the luxury of taking all the time you want to form a verbal masterpiece of research and discovery. The fact is that there is never enough time to write in the professional and commercial world without the nagging pressure of deadlines. So what do you do about it? Exactly what is it that you think about before you write? There are basically four areas to consider before you do anything:

1. Establish your writing objective.
2. Identify your readers.
3. Determine the scope of your writing project.
4. Perform the necessary research.

2.1.1 Establish Your Writing Objective

Technical writing objectives fall into three broad categories: instructive technical procedures, descriptive technical information, and general conveyance of technical information for managerial purposes.

These three categories are not always separate and distinct. An operations manual for a computerized machining center will have a mix of both descriptive and instructive procedures. That same manual may or may not include general managerial information. A report describing a malfunction in an aircraft's instrument panel will certainly contain descriptive information and managerial information. The report will not have instructions on how to fly an aircraft, however.

Once the general objective is clear, you must develop it into a specific objective. It is all too common for writers to determine a general direction and go no further. This leads to vague writing that is unclear in its intent.

Write the objective out. Don't try to have it in your head and pull it up from your memory when you need to refer to it. Write it out and examine it. By doing this, you can see whether the objective fits the writing task.

Don't stop with generalities. Make the objective specific. Written out, this objective tells you in one sentence exactly where you are going with the writing. The following objective is too general:

> To describe the effects of using sodium sulfite in film processing.

A better objective would be the following:

> To show the effects on high-speed coarse-grained film processing when combining sodium sulfite with the three leading black-and-white film developers (name the three) on the commercial market.

2.1.2 Identify Your Readers

When you identify your readers, don't simply identify whether they are technical, managerial, or general (or a combination of these three). Regardless of what general category your readers fall into, you must specifically determine their levels of understanding.

What do your readers need to know?

How deeply do you need to go into the subject? Is it an in-depth study or is it a relatively brief and simple memo-report? This determines the scope of the writing. It is not simply a matter of *how much* to write but *what specifically* to write about in terms of your readers' needs.

An operational staff studying a user's manual for operating a mainframe computer system needs information on how to operate the computer and what it will do for them. They don't need to know how it is programmed or how to service the system.

What do your readers already know?

Is this about an ongoing project in which everyone is involved, or is it a new project about which your readers know little or nothing? How much background information can you take for granted that they already know?

In the instance of a user's manual for a mainframe computer, we must assume that the readers know next to nothing about how to operate the system. If, however, the manual is for programmers working on the system, we can take for granted that they understand the computer languages such as COBOL or FORTRAN. By contrast, the user does not need to know programming language to operate the system.

Will jargon be understood?

Engineers who work in cellular communication understand "hand-off" very differently than a football coach understands "hand-off." If the communication is a field report directed to the engineering manager, the jargon will be understood. If, however, the football coach just bought a new carphone and read this term in the instruction manuals, it would not be understood. Jargon is a great shortcut only when it is understood.

Remember that jargon is exclusive language, understood only by a narrow margin of readers. This does not necessarily make jargon bad, but it does make it risky if your reader is not in that narrow margin of understanding. You must know and understand your readers to effectively use jargon. If you cannot discern this about your reader's understanding, replace the jargon with commonly understood and defined statements. For example, consider the following sentence:

> As yet, there are still several glitches in the software.

If the underlined jargon is replaced, the sentence reads as follows:

> As yet, the software is still giving out several wrong responses.

People involved in the computer software industry would talk in terms of "glitches" and not in lay terms of "wrong responses." Jargon affords a shortcut if understood, but to the general or lay reader more common words will be needed.

Short reports and memos that are directed to a small group of readers within a department of a computer company would most likely have little problem with jargon such as "boot up," "de-bug," "glitch," "I/O," "ports," or "bus." The owner of a new PC (personal computer) is more than likely to struggle with these terms if they are used throughout the user's manual.

How much definition will be required with the terminology?

Jargon and technical terminology overlap each other. Jargon can be replaced with common language and definition, but technical terminology must be defined. You must, however, be careful to define technical terms based on your readers' level of understanding. General readers will need to have most or all technical terms defined at least once. Graduate engineers, on the other hand, may not need to have any of the terms defined if they are within their area of expertise. (See Section 3.1.1 for more information on definition.)

Are your primary readers technical?

If technical readers are your audience, are they primarily theorists or are they technicians? If they are theorists, are you addressing their needs at the theoretical, scientific level? On the other hand, if your readers are primarily technicians at the practical level, are you addressing their needs from an applied, practical standpoint?

Are your primary readers managerial?

Managerial readers need a far more general approach that deals with the essence of a project and the managerial circumstances surrounding it. At what level of managerial authority are your readers? Are there a number of different levels of line authority involved as well as technical and nontechnical levels? If so, you must write at the level most common to your readers.

Are your readers primarily general-interest readers?

General-interest readers are the most difficult to identify specifically, because they can span so many different levels of technical understanding. This is especially true of manuals directed toward customers of technical products. When it comes to customers, you cannot take anything for granted. You must write to the level that is your best estimation of the lowest common denominator of technical understanding and expertise.

2.1.3 Determine the Scope of the Writing

You must know how deeply to go into your subject before you start writing. This depth or amount of detail is known as the *scope* of the piece of writing. You must determine this in the early planning stages of the writing.

Your writing objective and mix of readers will determine the depth and detail you must use. The scope varies a great deal depending on your judgment and the specific task at hand. Consequently, it is imperative that you be as exact and specific with your objective and reader profile as possible. By determining the scope of your writing project, you set the stage for research.

2.1.4 Research

Research is the process of gathering factual information. In the academic world, research is primarily done at the campus library. In the professional world, it is primarily a matter of calling upon experience and experimentation. These generally reflect primary research and secondary research.

Primary research is research you do yourself. If you take a trip to troubleshoot a series of manufacturing sites and draw conclusions, you have done primary research. If you put together a questionnaire and send it out and then receive replies, you have done primary research. If you do original scientific experiments and discover some new facts, you have done primary research.

The following are typical examples of primary research:

- Experiments
- Mail questionnaires
- Personal interviews
- Telephone interviews
- Personal observation/experience

Primary research is the most common type of research done in professional scientific and industrial settings.

Secondary research is research someone has done before you. If you go to the library and find information in the resource books, you are doing secondary research. If you refer to something that you read in *Scientific American*, you are doing secondary research. If you saw it in *The Wall Street Journal*, you are using secondary research. The following are typical examples of secondary research:

- Books
- Periodicals
- Newspapers
- Government documents
- Industrial and trade directories
- Published results of experiments

Secondary research is the most common type of research done at the academic level.

2.2 Organizing and Developing Your Writing

Understandable writing must be organized and then developed. Technical writing that rambles on without a clear destination will fail. You must have a purpose that is quickly discernible to the reader. This is why organizing your concepts and then working them into a method of development are so important. Technical writing must have an obvious structure. Where this structure becomes most pronounced is in instructional procedures. Instructions must be performed in a definite sequence to be effective. Instructions for building a house that start with the roof and work down to the foundation will cause the carpenters and bricklayers grave problems.

When you organize your writing, you work it into a method of development that will best serve your writing objective and your mix of readers. There are many ways to develop technical writing. The following methods of development are common in contemporary technical writing.

2.2.1 General to Specific Development

This form of development takes a general statement, concept, or position and then moves toward the specific elements that support this general position. Exhibit 2–1 is a typical example of general to specific development in technical writing.

Exhibit 2–1
General to Specific Deductive Development in Technical Writing

Relative humidity is the percentage of moisture in the air compared to its maximum capability to hold moisture under the same conditions. Seventy degree air can hold more than 12 times as much moisture as 10 degree air. Outside air at 10 degrees and 70 percent relative humidity drops to 7 percent relative humidity when heated to normal room temperature without other internal sources of moisture, such as cooking, laundry, showers, etc. That's only a fraction of the humidity recommended for the average heated home, and it's this "desert dryness" that makes you feel uncomfortable and takes moisture from your home, furnishings—even you and your family. The recommended indoor relative humidity is 35 percent and up to 45 percent in warmer climates or where special construction prevails—and not all humidifiers have the capacity to reach these levels.	**General**
Doctors often times have mentioned dry air as one of the causes for nose, throat, and other physical aggravations.	**Specific**
Heated air dries out and shrinks wood framing around doors and window frames. Gaps occur, permitting cold outside air infiltration. Heat loss and higher heating costs are often the result.	**Specific**
Heated, parched air causes separation of wood in floors, trim, and furniture ... excessive wear of fabrics and carpets ... loss of piano tone quality ... wall and ceiling cracks ... plant damage and annoying static shocks are also a by-product of dry air.	**Specific**
Proper humidity reduces heating costs by stopping wood shrinkage, which reduces cold air infiltration around door and window frames.	**Specific**
In turn, you'll feel warm at lower temperatures. You can actually dial down your thermostat and still be comfortable.	**Specific**

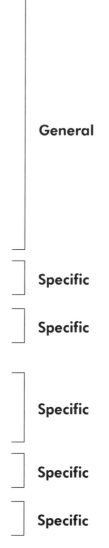

In cases where excessive dry air has been the cause of physical aggravations, doctors have prescribed whole-house humidification.	**Specific**
Furnishings are protected with proper humidity too—reducing the damaging effects of heated, parched air upon everything from your wood floors to your plants.	**Specific**

Source: Research Products Corporation.

2.2.2 Specific to General Development

This form of development takes specific statements, concepts, or positions and combines them to form a whole. This is the opposite direction of general to specific in that the specifics are combined to come out with the general conclusion. Exhibit 2–2 is a typical example of the specific to general form of development in technical writing.

2.2.3 Chronological Development

Chronological development is based on time. Events or procedures are normally shown in terms of their occurrence. The time sequence normally reflects past-present-future or future-present-past. Remember that this type of development is only effective if the *time sequence* is the most important element.

This type of development is used often in the highly theoretical and scientific fields where historically documenting the development or progress of technology is concerned. In the following example at the bottom of page 35, major technological advancements during the Middle Ages are put into historical perspective by using a chronological pattern of development.

Exhibit 2–2
Specific to General Development in Technical Writing

The paint spray booth is an important element of the finishing operation. If properly engineered and installed and efficiently maintained, the booth provides an efficient and safe working environment for the operators. It does this by drawing particulate and vapors away from the painter. The exhaust also keeps overspray away from products already finished, assuring better finish quality.	**Specific**
Spray booth designs and overspray collection are being closely scrutinized by government regulatory agencies such as OSHA and EPA and city, county, and state regulatory bodies. The selection and installation of a spray booth must be undertaken with the approval of the appropriate agencies.	**Specific**
Changes in chemical coatings and their method of application often result in significant modification of the spray booth and the overspray collection system. Many of the new coating materials are more expensive. The equipment to apply these coatings is more sophisticated. Industry is looking for methods to apply the coatings with maximum transfer efficiency.	**Specific**
Four out of five new booths sold today are equipped with dry filters as the means of collecting overspray. As the industry moves more and more to high-solids coatings, water-borne coatings, and powder coatings, while the coating application method puts more of the coating onto the product, the use of dry-filter overspray-collection systems should continue to increase.	**General**

Source: Reprinted with permission. © 1984 Gardner Publications, Inc. and Research Products Corporation.

Significant Advances in Technology in the Middle Ages

1. A.D. 1000 to 1100:
   — Astrolabe and lanteen sail
   — Stamping and hammer mills

- Gunpowder used in warfare
- Movable type in printing

2. A.D. 1100 to 1200:
   - Sternpost rudder replaces steering oar
   - Papermaking
   - Woodcuts used for initial letters
   - Manufacture of silk
3. A.D. 1200 to 1300:
   - Introduction of "cog" cargo vessel
   - English longbow
   - Spectacles
   - Wheelbarrow
   - Distilling techniques
   - Minting gold coins
   - Coal mining
4. A.D. 1300 to 1400:
   - Wind-driven tower mills
   - Sluices, locks, and weirs
   - Steel crossbow, artillery, plate armor
   - Silk mills
5. A.D. 1400 to 1500:
   - Development of military technology
   - Development of navigational technology
   - Efficient clocks developed
   - Gutenberg applies movable type

2.2.4 Sequential Development

This is a method of development in which the order of events determines the structure of the writing. The order or sequence will depend on what criteria are used to set up the sequence. Order of importance or necessity are two likely sequences. Process descriptions and technical instructions are the most common types of writing to use this type of development (see Sections 3.1.3 and 3.1.4). The following example shows the sequential order of development for processing a photographic print. The sequence is absolutely necessary for the process to work.

The Process of Making Photographic Enlargements

1. In darkness or "safe" light, a sheet of photographic print paper is removed from a light-safe container and placed under the enlarger (a type of vertical projector).
2. In darkness or "safe" light, the image is enlarged and exposed onto the print paper with the enlarger.
3. In darkness or "safe" light, the exposed print is submerged in developer until the positive image appears.
4. In darkness or "safe" light, the print is next submerged in stop bath briefly to stop the development action on the emulsion.
5. In darkness or "safe" light, the print is next submerged in fixer solution to chemically make the image permanent and light "safe."
6. In complete light, the print is rinsed under running water to remove excess fixer.
7. The print is dried off.

2.2.5 Cause and Effect

This is a method of development that emphasizes a process in which one element causes the next. It does not matter whether you start with the cause and move to the effect or, conversely, start with the effect and explain it with the cause. You can also approach this method from a single cause and a single effect to any combination and number of causes and effects.

Highly scientific and highly technical experiments and processes usually depend on this type of development for explanation and definition. The following example uses cause and effect to explain a scientific principle.

The Doppler Effect

The Doppler effect was discovered by and named after Christian Doppler in 1842. It states that apparent changes in wave frequency take place relative to the motion of the wave source and observer. [cause]

Sound is a familiar and typical wave source subject to the Doppler effect. If you are standing at a railroad crossing and an approaching train sounds its horn at a constant rate as it passes you, the pitch of the horn rises as the train approaches and descends after it passes. The sound of the horn changes from your vantage point but remains constant in pitch from the vantage point of a person in the train. [effect]

Light is also a wave source and subject to the Doppler effect. It is through this effect that the movement of distant stars can be approximated. If a star is moving toward the earth, there is a shift in the color spectrum toward blue. If the star is moving away from the earth, there is a shift in the color spectrum toward red. These changes in the color spectrum are the results of the Doppler effect on light waves. [effect]

2.2.6 Comparison

This method of development shows how things are alike as well as different from each other. It is especially useful in explaining unfamiliar concepts by comparing the new concept to a familiar one. In other cases, it may be a simple matter of presenting various types of objects or processes and comparing their characteristics.

Remember first that you must have a basis for comparison. This basis can be anything from cost to strength to reliability. A basis of comparison could also be a combination of things such as cost versus reliability. The following example compares a wing nut to a hexagonal nut. Both are a part of everyday mechanical fasteners, but they are strikingly different in their application.

The Hexagonal Nut Compared to the Wing Nut

A wing nut has "wings" or handles on the sides that can be gripped by hand to tighten or loosen.

A hexagonal nut has six flat sides forming a hexagonal shape that can be gripped with pliers or a wrench.

A wing nut goes on screws that are in the open and that can be easily grasped with the hands. Wing nuts need a lot of room for clearance of the wings and the hands turning them.

A hexagonal nut can go on screws within the tight confines of machinery or other applications where economy of spacc is needed.

A wing nut can only be tightened to the amount of torque that the human hand can perform.

A hexagonal nut can be tightened to a high degree of torque delivered with such tools as pliers, wrenches, or pneumatic tools.

Wing nuts are best suited to applications where the nut is frequently loosened and tightened by hand.

Hexagonal nuts are best suited to applications that require a high degree of torque and an economy of space.

2.2.7 Spatial Development

This development method relates to the position and space that physical elements occupy. This type of development is crucial in the description of mechanisms and how their parts interrelate and operate. It is also an integral element of buildings and machines with their relative layout and physical proximities to one another. Exhibit 2–3 shows the design elements of three types paint spray booths. Notice that the explanation of each type of booth depends on a spatial development of the design description.

2.3 The Outline

2.3.1 The Value of Outlining

An outline has much the same use to the technical writer that a map has to the serious traveler. You would not start to drive from Bangor to Los Angeles without giving a lot of consideration to the route you

Exhibit 2–3
Spatial Development in Technical Writing

TYPE 1 — THE TOTALLY ENCLOSED BOOTH

This booth has sides, a floor and a ceiling (Fig. 1). Therefore, if 100 fpm of air is moving past the gun and the operator, then the same velocity of air is moving through the RP Paint Arrestor bank.

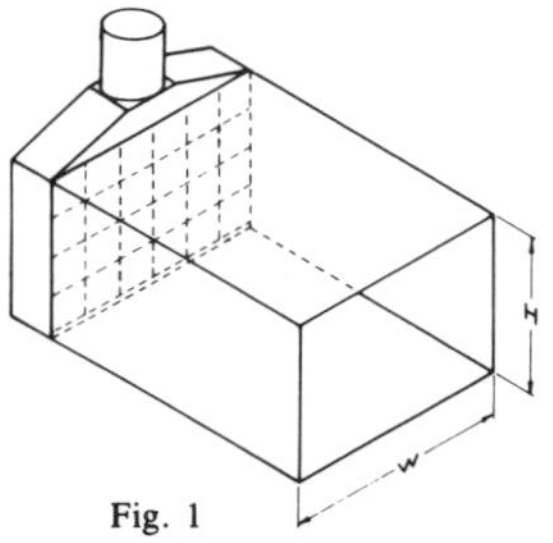

Fig. 1

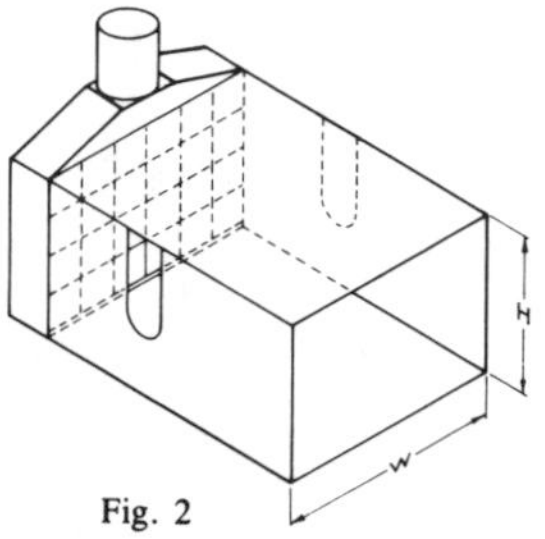

Fig. 2

TYPE 2 — THE ENCLOSED BOOTH WITH CONVEYOR OPENINGS

This booth is similar to Type 1 except that openings are cut in the walls through which the conveyor line and the objects being sprayed move (Fig. 2). In addition to the 100 fpm moving past the operator, some air will come in through the openings.

Therefore, it will be necessary to move 125-150 fpm through the RP Paint Arrestor bank to maintain the 100 fpm minimum past the operator.

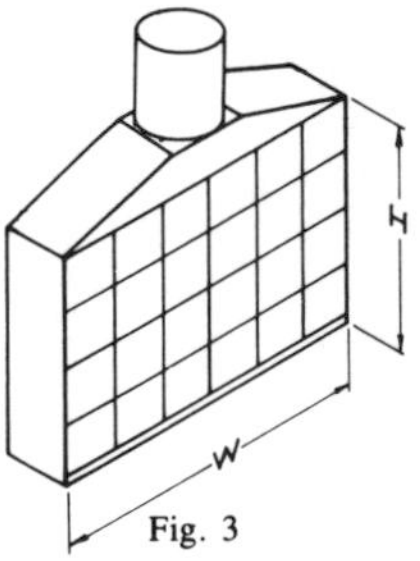

Fig. 3

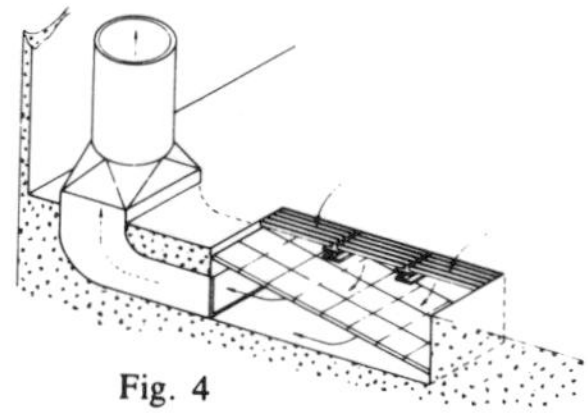

Fig. 4

TYPE 3 — THE OPEN BOOTH

This booth has no sides. It may be a wall type (Fig. 3) or it may be a downdraft (Fig. 4). Air passing through the RP Paint Arrestor bank not only comes past the operator but moves in from all areas. It will, therefore, be necessary to maintain 300-350 fpm through the RP Arrestor media to maintain 100 fpm past the face of an operator standing approximately 5-6 ft. from the media bank.

Source: Research Products Corporation.

are going to take. Like the serious traveler, the serious technical writer also requires a map.

You also need a route in order to get where you are going in your writing. The route you take is your method of development. The actual physical map that you will use is your outline. Both are absolutely crucial to success as a technical writer. Like a map, your outline will help you in a number of different ways. Consider the following ways that an outline helps a writer:

1. It forces parallel structure of your ideas.
2. It allows for easy evaluation of your organization and development.
3. It shows you completeness.
4. It saves you time.

Outlining forces parallel structure of your ideas.

When you write an outline, you set your method of development down in a parallel structure. The very act of outlining forces this. This simply means that ideas of equal importance get equal emphasis. Ideas of lesser importance are always subordinate to some idea of greater importance and related to that idea. Consider the following example:

I. First Main Idea
   A. First subtopic subordinate to I
   B. Second subtopic subordinate to I
II. Second Main Idea

In this example, there are four elements. All are parallel, and two are subordinate. The first main idea and the second main idea (I and II) are parallel. They will receive equal emphasis and are of equal importance. The second main idea is not subordinate to the first main idea, however. They are both designated with a Roman numeral and are flush with each other in the column, which indicates a parallel set of ideas. The fact that "I" precedes "II" simply means that based on the organizational method the idea in "I" should come before the idea in "II." They are both equally important and receive equal emphasis.

Also parallel are "A" and "B." These two subtopics are also subordinate to "I." This simply means that like "I" and "II," they will receive equal emphasis and importance in the writing, and they both depend on and relate directly to "I."

Outlining allows for easy evaluation of your organization and development.

This aspect of outlining has a dual advantage. Not only can you evaluate your approach to your writing assignment, but anyone who must pass approval on the writing project can give preliminary approval. This has tremendous value in speeding up the process of revising, correcting, and rewriting. If you look at the previous example, you can tell at a glance where everything is situated logically. If, while looking over an outline, you notice a violation of logic or fact, you can make the change far easier and faster than trying to pick it out of the finished text.

Outlining shows you completeness.

There is nothing worse than trying to write something and getting to the end of it only to realize that you have left something out. Even though word processing allows you to move or add copy to other locations, you still must rework transitions and make sure that what you had to move or add fits smoothly. Outlining allows you to do this quickly and easily, because you have not yet written anything at this stage. You can spot the problem quickly and make the addition or deletion easily.

Outlining saves you time.

This is probably the greatest value in outlining and, ironically, the most overlooked. Most who neglect outlining do so in order to save time. The fact is that they actually cause themselves more undue and time-consuming rewriting.

Writers who outline as a regular, systematic procedure save themselves time because the outline will point out defects clearly and allow their repair long before they are in final prose. After all, if you don't have time to do it right the first time, you most certainly don't have time to do it over again. By not taking the time to write an outline, you probably are causing yourself the inconvenience and aggravation of time-consuming rewrites.

2.3.2 Outline Formats

When you format technical writing, you are deciding on the actual physical form and appearance that it will have on paper. There are basically three ways to format an outline. However, there are probably an infinite number of combinations of these three. What is important is getting some kind of a physical outline down on paper to use as a guide for your writing. You can't outline something in your mind. You must write it down on paper and follow it as you write. The three basic types of outline are as follows:

1. Simple list
2. Academic outline
3. Engineering outline

Simple List

This is the simplest form of outlining. It will suffice for all brief and simple written communications, such as memos and brief letters. Even though these types of writing seem so simple as to not require outlining, it is amazing to find out how often the simple memo has left out needed information such as time, place, or someone's name. This is why even these simple and brief messages should be outlined at least in a simple list form.

The greatest advantages of a list are speed and simplicity. It is an outline that you can write simply and quickly for a routine message. Its main disadvantage is that it does not allow for complex ideas. Be careful not to use this for any writing that requires more than a simple parallel structure. Consider the following example of the listing technique:

Memorandum

1. Announce meeting at 2:00 P.M.
2. Have section heads bring weekly reports.
3. Mention change in travel policy.

This list is for a very simple memo. It allows the writer to see the order and the content of the three points to be written in the memo.

Academic Outline

An academic outline is one of two types of formal outline formats. This particular type is called "academic" mainly because it is the kind of outline format most commonly taught in high schools and colleges. It uses a combination of Roman numerals, Arabic numerals, and uppercase and lowercase English letters.

This format has the advantage of distinctly separating the various parallel structures in the outline. The structures are easily separated because the Roman numerals, letters, and Arabic numbers are distinct. You can see the divisions at a glance. The only disadvantage is that if you go beyond a fourth level of parallel subordination, you must either repeat a symbol previously used or make up a new one. The following is the format of a typical academic outline:

I. Main Heading
    A. First subtopic under main heading
    B. Second subtopic under main heading
        1. First subtopic under B
        2. Second subtopic under B
            a. First subtopic under 2
            b. Second subtopic under 2
II. Main Heading

Engineering Outline

The engineering outline is also frequently referred to as a *decimal outline* because of the decimal points that separate each entry. This can be a little misleading, however, because the decimal points do not actually refer to any fractional element in the mathematical sense. Consequently, the term *engineering* is more appropriate. It is called an *engineering outline* because of its almost exclusive use in the scientific and engineering communities.

This outline format has the advantage of being able to go to any level of complexity of detail without repeating symbols. Because of the meticulous detail many engineering and scientific reports need, this advantage is a real one. Another advantage is the immediate ability to number all levels of the actual prose in accordance with the outline. In many high-tech companies, even the paragraphs in a technical manual or report are numbered (as in this text). In each case a reference to the paragraph number will take you directly to the same point in the outline and research documentation.

Consider the following example of a typical engineering outline:

1 Main Heading
  1.1 First subtopic under 1
  1.2 Second subtopic under 1
    1.2.1 First subtopic under 1.2
    1.2.2 Second subtopic under 1.2
      1.2.2.1 First subtopic under 1.2.2
      1.2.2.2 Second subtopic under 1.2.2
2 Main Heading

2.3.3 The Three Basic Outline Styles

There are three styles of outline, and each has its distinct advantages and disadvantages. The divisions are based on how closely you need to approximate your actual prose before writing the draft. These three styles are as follows:

1. Topical outline
2. Sentence outline
3. Paragraph outline

Topical Outline

A topical outline uses only topic headings or short phrases for each outline entry. Because it is quickly written and easy to use, it is the choice for brief and fairly straightforward types of writing such as memos, letters, and short memo-reports. By outlining in brief topic form, you have very little problem with adding, deleting, or moving topics to other locations in the paper.

The disadvantage with this type of outline is that it is not detailed. If this type is used for a large and detailed communication, you will not remember all of the details concerned with each topic entry. You must then constantly refer back to notes or your memory.

Sentence Outline

A sentence outline has each entry in the form of a complete sentence. The discipline of a complete sentence forces you to think in greater detail about the outline entry. The obvious advantage is that greater detail makes for easier memory of detail when you write the draft.

The disadvantage with this type of outline is that you may be tempted to string the outline sentences together into a choppy prose and call that the written report. You must do more than string skeletal sentences together to create interesting and informative writing. This will be explained in detail in Section 2.4 on writing the rough draft.

Paragraph Outline

The paragraph outline has all the *main* entries summarized with a complete paragraph. All subordinate entries are then structured as complete sentences. This type of outline is the most complete and comprehensive approach to technical writing you can take. You may choose to use paragraph outlines when it comes to extensive and detailed writings of considerable length such as full manuals and extensive project completion reports.

The major advantage of a paragraph outline is its capacity for detail and completeness. This outline leaves little or nothing to memory later on. It will lead you through your draft with more ease than any other type of outline.

Its primary disadvantage is the time-consuming detail of the writing. You can't write this outline in a hurry and then fire off the piece of writing just in time to meet a deadline. This approach to outlining and writing takes a timely and disciplined approach. It shares the disadvantage of the sentence outline in that you still must write a draft to create readable prose.

2.4 The Rough Draft

The first draft you write is the *rough draft*. This is the only draft that you write without the help of revision. This draft comes out of your head with only the help of your outline. Any other draft has the benefit of at least partial revision of the actual prose.

2.4.1 How to Write a Rough Draft

If this draft turns out any other way than rough, you did it wrong. This is the one time you do not clutter your mind with the mechanical elements of technical writing. The only thing you are striving to do at this point is to turn the outline into prose. To do this, you take everything in your head concerning each outline point and put it on paper in rough form. Just get it down. That is your *only* concern.

Speed is essential. Don't labor over the writing. Don't wait for "inspiration." Start putting words on paper no matter how poorly written they may seem to you. The faster you write, the easier it is for your mind to quit worrying about how "good" or "bad" it may be.

Don't stop to correct. With the advent of PCs and word processing, it is especially tempting to move the cursor back and correct types and minor mistakes. This is the worst thing you can do, because it will bog down your thinking process. Remind yourself that this is the first draft and not the last draft. There will be ample time and other drafts for correction—but not on this draft.

2.4.2 The Rough Draft Cures Writer's Block

The rough draft is the major cure for writer's block, because it gets you started writing, no matter what. People get writer's block because they don't know what to say or how to say it in writing. An outline shows you what you have to say. The rough draft shows you how to say it without worrying about how. You just do it. If it isn't "good," don't worry. There is a place for revision and correction in the next step.

Do not show anyone your rough draft. Show them your outline or any subsequent drafts after the rough draft—but not the rough draft. There is a very good reason for this. By absolutely not showing anyone your rough draft, you have the assurance that no one but you will ever know exactly how bad you write on your first effort. This has the effect of loosening up your mind and putting it at ease so it can just concentrate on getting the ideas into writing from the outline.

From time to time you will hear the expression *creative writing*. This expression is usually reserved for fiction and poetry. The fact is that all writing, including technical writing, is creative writing in the sense that no one says anything exactly like anyone else. When you write the rough draft, you are doing creative writing because no one will turn an outline into raw prose in exactly the same way as someone else. Once it is down on paper, it is exactly you. The only thing left for you to do is to correct it and shape it into good technical prose.

2.5 Revision

If you have carefully followed the system to this point, you are now ready to revise your writing. Revision is not simply a matter of correcting spelling errors and placing commas. Revision is a matter of converting your raw creative prose into flowing and readable writing.

Like so many other parts of the writing process, it too has a system. The system is basically made up of three parts:

1. Activate the writing
2. Clarify the writing
3. Simplify the writing

These three steps will turn your technical writing into finished prose that flows with clarity and conciseness.

The order in which you perform the three will naturally vary from writer to writer. You must perform these three steps when you revise, and you should perform them in this order.

2.5.1 Activate the Language

Active, lively writing is at the core of interest and understanding. The central element to active written language is your use of verbs. In technical writing, your verbs must show action and life. They must do things rather than simply skirt the issues and talk around things. Keep a lean and direct approach to your verb use. Always ask yourself whether there is direct action involved in your sentences.

There are two main elements involved in activating language:

1. Check active voice and passive voice.
2. Activate suppressed verbs.

Check active voice and passive voice.

As mentioned earlier in this manual, the use of the active voice is the keystone of clear, concise technical writing. Your first editing concern must be for use of the active voice. As a general rule, you will find that most of your sentences will need to be converted from a passive voice construction to an active voice construction.

When you edit for the active voice, don't concentrate on the content. Instead, read the sentences for their wording. If you have the wording and the verb form as primary to your interest, the active and passive constructions will seem to jump right out at you. Frequent use of the verb *to be* linked with participles of other verbs is a sure sign of the passive voice. In most cases these forms will be the passive voice and should be converted to the active voice.

Be ruthless about changing the passive voice to active voice. Remember that it is far easier to change a few active voice constructions back to the passive voice for variety than it is to keep trying to activate.

The following are some typical changes from passive to active:

Stress is exerted by the load pushing down on the platform. [passive]

The load exerts stress on the platform by pushing down on it. [active]

First, the electrical energy input of the motor must be figured. [passive]

First you must figure the electrical energy input of the motor. [active]

Activate suppressed verbs.

Suppressed (weak) verbs are constructions that have held the verb forms back from their most effective expression. This type of construction is usually suppressing the active voice, but not always. Depending on the context, it can also be a passive construction.

Word endings such as "-tion," "-ing," "-ent," and the use of prepositional phrases with verb forms are your best clues to suppressed verbs. These usages signal wordiness that is suppressing verbs from "acting" instead of "being."

The following are some typical suppressed verbs with the appropriate corrections:

Completion of the heat tests has been accomplished by the lab. [*completion* is suppressed]

The lab has completed the heat tests. [activated]

The fluorescent lighting is dependent on a dedicated generation system for its operation. [*operation* is suppressed]

A dedicated generation system operates the fluorescent lighting system. [activated]

2.5.2 Clarify the Writing

If your reader can't understand what you are writing, you've failed. When your writing is clear, your reader can go directly to your ideas and concepts without struggling with the writing.

To achieve this clarity, you should check some primary elements of your writing and correct them when needed. The order in which you check them is up to you, but you must specifically check for all of them. The revision elements that lead to clarity in writing are the following:

1. Decide on personal versus impersonal reference.
2. Use connotation and denotation.
3. Determine whether jargon is helpful.
4. Change abstract words to concrete words.
5. Eliminate affected language.
6. Replace clichés and trite language.
7. Correct misplaced modifiers.

Decide on personal versus impersonal reference.

Technical writing tends to lean toward impersonal reference far more than any other type of writing. There is almost a fear of ever using the pronouns *you*, *I*, or *we*. The taboo against first-person (I) and second-person (you) references in technical writing is old and difficult to overcome.

The roots of this preference for the impersonal reference to the actor seem to be in the emphasis on the technical findings, results, or experiments rather than on the performer of these actions. This preference does not hold up, however, when put to the test of clarity and directness. A strict adherence to the impersonal approach in writing actually begs for passivity in verbs and lack of clarity because of the actor's obscurity.

When you switch from the traditional impersonal to the personal use of pronouns, you allow a much easier approach to clear, active writing. This use of the first- and second-person pronouns in no way hurts the writing other than to break with the traditional. Consider the following examples:

Impersonal passive: Tensile strength tests were made.
Personal active: We made the necessary tensile strength tests.

You as the writer must make the decision whether to use first- and second-person reference or to deal only in the impersonal. Realistically speaking, many organizations (perhaps your own) absolutely demand the impersonal. If this is the case, you can still write actively and clearly by simply altering your approach to the impersonal. In the following construction, the impersonal approach has been maintained but still activated into lively writing.

Impersonal but active: The necessary tensile strength tests showed that . . .

Use connotation and denotation.

Words are the basic units of our written language. Words not only have basic meanings that are categorized in the dictionary, but they also have meanings based on the feelings they provoke. If you are considering the basic dictionary meaning of a word, you are dealing with its denotative meaning. If, however, you are primarily considering the feelings and emotions received from the use of a certain word, you are dealing with its connotative meaning.

In technical writing, the more you move toward connotation, the more risk you take that your meaning will not be clear. The difficulty is in the fact that no word is completely free of connotative meaning. As a result, careful choice of words becomes paramount to making your message clear. The following are examples of common words and their more connotative counterparts:

- waste —junk
- miscellany —odds and ends
- things —stuff
- offspring —kids

- man — guy
- woman — gal
- compact — smash

Determine whether jargon is helpful.

Jargon is exclusive language and vocabulary. Every organization has its own sub-language or jargon. When a person first comes into a new job or organization, he or she must "learn the language." Jargon is exclusive because the language is coded to mean other than what it would seem to mean denotatively. Only the members of the group understand the *actual* meaning. As soon as the underlying meaning becomes known to a vast number of people, it is no longer jargon.

Jargon has an advantage and disadvantage, and both stem from its exclusivity. On the one hand, jargon is an abbreviated language that makes for quick and easy messages. When you use jargon in your written or spoken communication, you take a shortcut. You don't have to explain or elaborate on the concepts or their expression. The disadvantage to jargon is that only an exclusive few understand the meaning. If you are not extremely careful in evaluating your audience, you will write a message that is at best unclear and sometimes totally misunderstood.

The broader and more far-reaching the writing, the greater the risk you take with jargon. Jargon can be a helpful tool in a memo of limited circulation and exclusive readership. However, a manual loaded with jargon that is going out to a wide range of customers could be a disaster of misunderstanding. A prime example of this type of mistake was the early days of the personal computer boom. The wide market of buyers could not understand the jargon of the experts who were trying to sell the computers. The following are examples of common computer jargon:

- boot up
- bit
- byte
- megs
- glitch
- I/O
- ports
- CPU

- ROM
- RAM
- DOS

These terms are exclusive to the world of computers. You must be familiar with that world to understand them. A computer novice would need definitions of all of them.

Change abstract words to concrete words.

Vague and abstract words obscure meaning in technical writing. They are words without precise meaning. Some of these words have such a broad meaning as to mean anything to anyone. Others are imprecise in the context of the writing in which they are used.

Make sure your technical writing is precise and concrete. The following examples show how abstract words can be replaced with concrete words:

The supports must be strong enough ... [abstract]

The supports must have a tensile strength of ... [concrete]

... 145 pieces of brass rod. [abstract]

... 145 lengths of 3/8" OD brass rod each 24" long. [concrete]

Eliminate affected language.

Affected language uses complex and impressive vocabulary and sentence constructions that say little. It is writing that attempts to sound official, legal, or scientific. Affected language is a great enemy of clarity. In technical writing, it is most important to write to express ideas and thoughts rather than to impress your reader with your importance or position. One clue that writing is intended to impress rather than express is this affected language.

Consider the following typical examples of pompous, bombastic, and affected language:

- admonish —warn
- altercation —dispute

- anathema — curse
- approximately — about
- ascertain — find out
- compunction — regret
- contiguous — touching
- convoluted — twisted
- countermand — cancel
- edification — benefit
- elucidate — make clear
- expedite — hurry along
- facile — easy
- innocuous — harmless
- oblique — indirect
- periphery — outer edge
- remuneration — pay
- stringent — strict
- subsequently — later
- surreptitiously — secretly
- tenuous — twisting
- ulterior — hidden
- utilize — use

Replace clichés and trite language.

Trite language that is riddled with clichés interferes with clarity and is irritating to your reader. Elongated forms of words, superficial use of foreign words, and idiomatic expressions all add to this enemy of clarity.

Consider the following examples and their corrections of typical clichés and trite forms of language:

- At this point in time — presently
- consensus of opinion — consensus
- during the course of — during
- in the vast majority of cases — in most cases
- on a weekly basis — weekly
- refer back to — refer to
- until such time as — until
- due to the fact that — due to/because
- very necessary — necessary
- in spite of the fact that — despite

Correct misplaced modifiers.

Gerunds, participles, and infinitives are all verbals that are frequently used in phrases to add further information or meaning to sentences. The problem is when their placement in the sentence confuses rather than clarifies. When they are obvious, dangling modifiers can be amusing:

> Jack and Jill found a dollar walking to the store. [We know who was actually walking to the store.]

The problem is that most dangling modifiers are not obvious and can create problems that are far from amusing. To solve the problem of a dangling modifier, simply stop it from "dangling." You do this by placing it nearest the element you want it to modify. Consider the following example:

> The topic of the seminar was digital conversion of analogue systems at our Chicago branch.
>
> The topic of the seminar at our Chicago branch was digital conversion of analogue systems.

Either of these statements is plausible. Only the writer would know which of them is correct.

2.5.3 Simplify the Writing

There is a big difference between simplified writing and simple-minded writing. To simplify technical writing is not necessarily to condescend in your written approach. Your readers want to get to your ideas as easily as possible. They don't want to work any harder at it than they have to. Why should they? It stands to reason that wherever you can simplify, you make it easier for your reader.

The following elements are basic to the simplification process in revision:

1. Keep down sentence length.
2. Keep down word length.
3. Eliminate needless words.
4. Simplify positive and negative constructions.
5. Watch out for the "It . . . that" syndrome.

Keep down sentence length.

Long sentences are hard to read. The longer the sentence, the more you limit your reader's ability to understand. The reason long sentences are difficult to read is that there is more for your reader to keep track of and assimilate in one complete thought. By the time your readers get to the end of a 30-word sentence, they will be lucky if they remember the beginning of the sentence.

Where this problem really begins to take its toll is in the complete piece made up of many sentences. If one sentence was all your readers had to keep track of, then maybe a 30–50-word sentence would not be such a disaster. For one thing, they could spend more time deciphering what that sentence is about. When the writing is clogged with sentence after sentence of inordinate length, it is then that the writing becomes more than readers are willing to digest.

Compound, complex, and compound-complex sentences contain many words and should be used sparingly. They have their place, but an overdose of them can take its toll on readers. Try to break these types of sentences into simple, declarative sentences. Longer and more complex sentences make for variety and sometimes are needed to adequately express a thought.

You will find that your first draft will have many long sentences. This is because your mind is blocking in prose thoughts and tends to cram a lot of information into one sentence. In the first draft your mind tends to write passively rather than actively and thus will produce long and tedious sentences. Vigorously break these long sentences down and rewrite them in simpler constructions.

At this point it would be reasonable to ask just what a long, short, or medium sentence is. The length of sentences has to do with average sentence length. It should be evident that some will be short and some will be long, but the average length should be readable. If you have nothing but short, 4–5-word sentences, the writing will be choppy. On the other hand, 30–50-word sentences will bog your readers down. A good, readable length in technical writing falls in the range of 12–15 words per sentence.

Having been given this range, don't become dogmatic about it. This range is arbitrary and reflects a personal experience with technical articles and reports. Yours may vary from this. What is important is that in informational writing a declarative sentence is infinitely easier to understand than tomes of compound-complex, passive sentences. The following sentence is too long:

> The total quantity of air (Cubic Feet of air per Minute or CFM) to be moved is governed by various local and state codes and if no local or state codes exist, the total quantity of air (CFM) to be exhausted from the hood shall be determined by one of the formulas that follow.

Consider the same sentence after it is broken down into shorter and more easily read sentences:

> The total CFM (Cubic Feet of air movement per Minute) must usually conform to local or state code. If there is no code, you can figure the CFM by any one of the following formulas.

Keep down word length.

Like sentence length, word length plays an important role in the ease with which readers can get through the writing and into the concept. Word length here refers to the number of syllables rather than the number of letters in the word. Shorter words are one or two syllables; longer words are four or five syllables. Three syllables may or may not be long, depending on how common the word is.

It is here that technical writing presents a far more complicated issue than other types of writing. Technical writing always has a distinct vocabulary of technical terms for each specific technical discipline. The medical field has its own unique vocabulary compared with the vocabulary of mechanical engineering. It is important to remember that you can't dispense with technical terms. You may have to go to great lengths to make sure that they are understood, but you cannot get rid of them. What you can do is control the nontechnical vocabulary. It is in these words that syllable length will make for either easy or difficult reading. It is in the nontechnical vocabulary that you must be careful to monitor word length and to choose common words.

The most blatant example in recent years is the verb "utilize." It is almost impossible to find an instance where the verb "use" won't work better.

Eliminate needless words.

Get rid of needless words. In almost all cases, needless words are directly or indirectly redundant for the sake of impressiveness. Consider the following example and how the elimination of needless words has helped.

> Shipping considerations will be easy because of the flexible nature of the materials.
>
> Shipping will be easy because the materials are flexible.

Two particular problems with needless words crop up when you use *of* and when you use *the*. The problem is particularly difficult because neither is an optional word. When you use them correctly, they are absolutely necessary in the construction. When you use either of these two words unnecessarily, you complicate the writing.

Consider the following examples and their corrections using the words *of* and *the*:

- all of the labs — all labs
- many of the engineers — many engineers
- some of the tests — some tests
- the engineers at the test site — engineers at the test site

But always use *the*, however, if it is a *specific* reference such as the following:

She is *the engineer* who performed *the initial tests.*

Simplify positive and negative constructions.

Present positive statements and negative statements in their most simplified and direct construction. Technical writers tend to cause unnecessary complication due to the constructions they use. Making negative statements poses the greatest difficulty. For instance, don't use *were not a success* or *did not succeed* when *failed* makes the statement far more directly.

Consider the following examples of positive and negative statements and how they can be simplified to make direct, clear statements:

This project will not be delayed if the lab approves the latest series of tests.

This project will continue on schedule if the lab approves the latest series of tests.

Watch out for the "It . . . that" syndrome.

The "It . . . that" construction is the number-one problem with technical writing's overemphasis of the impersonal approach. You can always simplify this tangled approach to language by activating the verb and shortening the statement. Be alert to sentences that start with such phrases as:

It has been shown that ...

It can be proven that ...

It is a known fact that ...

These typical phrases are clues to this impersonal and wordy construction. The following examples show how to correct it:

It has been shown that the additive helps reduce frictional wear on parts.
[The additive helps reduce frictional wear on parts.]

It can be proven that the additive helps reduce frictional wear on parts.
[Tests prove the additive helps reduce frictional wear on parts.]

It is a known fact that the additive helps reduce frictional wear on parts.
[Facts show the additive helps reduce frictional wear on parts.]

2.6 The Final Draft

The actual physical form of your technical writing influences your readers before they ever read the first word. There are five basic steps that you must always take to ensure the attractiveness and sense of professionalism your technical writing deserves:

1. Allow for generous use of white space.
2. Use topic heads often.
3. Use listing.
4. Use illustrations effectively.
5. Include adequate appendixes.

2.6.1 Allow for Generous Use of White Space

There is nothing more discouraging to your reader than to look at a report that is solid copy in small print that covers every inch of the page. (This is why legal contracts are seldom if ever read.) A reader wants to look at a page and sense that it can be read with ease. Your reader does not want to be intimidated at the outset.

The key to having your reader want to read your writing is adequate white space. White space is the area on a page that has no printing or illustration on it. White space gives your reader a sense of ease about the writing as well as the figures or equations. It encourages rather than intimidates. Generous use of white space makes your reader want to read what you have written.

Consider the following two examples. The first example makes poor use of white space, and the second example makes effective use of white space.

> Manufacturers have prepared charts that show which of their models should be used with what carrier weight class. However, if you want to double-check those figures or match hammers and carriers already in the fleet, use this formula: the quantity of Wh multiplied by A divided by the quantity Wc multiplied by B where A equals the maximum reach of carrier, B equals half the length of the wheelbase, and Wc equals the weight of the carrier. Generally, if the ratio derived is less than 0.30, the carrier is too heavy. If the ratio is greater than 0.50, the breaker is too heavy.

> Manufacturers have prepared charts that show which of their models should be used with what carrier weight class. However, if you want to double-check those figures or match hammers and carriers already in the fleet, use this formula:
>
> $$\frac{A \times Wh}{B \times Wc}$$
>
> where:
>
> A = Maximum reach of carrier
> B = Half the length of the wheelbase

Wh = Weight of the breaker
Wc = Weight of the carrier

Generally, if the ratio derived is less than 0.30, the carrier is too heavy. If the ratio is greater than 0.50, the breaker is too heavy.

Source: Construction Equipment Magazine.

2.6.2 Use Topic Heads Often

Topic heads open up the copy and allow for the use of white space. Your readers are quickly discouraged with mountains of words with no breaks anywhere in sight. They need help penetrating this mountain of words, and they get that help from the topic heads.

Topic heads also act much like signs do on a highway. They allow your reader to know what is coming up next. Topic heads alert your readers to major breaks in the writing and in its concepts. Through the use of topic heads, your readers have the ability to move ahead in the writing and skim it or read it out of sequence.

Your reader can also move back through the writing with ease. There is nothing more frustrating than to go back in a novel and try to find a certain passage. There is nothing to help you find it unless you noted the page. Unlike a novel, much of technical writing is written with reference in mind. The topic headings make the reference to different points in the writing easy.

Notice how in the following example the topic heads not only break up the writing but also force white space onto the page:

SYSTEM DESCRIPTION

System Controls

Maintain Terminals

This online facility allows the System Administrator to add, amend, or delete Terminal details including System ID, Printers, and authorized Menus.

Maintain Operators

This online facility allows the System Administrator to add, amend, or delete operator details, including operator ID (User ID), name, password, default, menu, all Operator valid Conversations, and Warehouse Security.

Maintain Menus

This online facility allows the System Administrator to design new Menus or redefine existing Menus. For each option on the Menu, a Conversation Number, Description, and the associated Program Name should be entered. Where further security is required to protect a Conversation, a password can be specified.

Source: BACG, Inc.

2.6.3 Use Listing

Listing saves your reader time and makes it far easier to see what the various elements of the list are. Without using a list, the items would often become a cumbersome block of information that would be next to impossible to follow or understand.

Like white space and topic headings, lists that are set off from the main block of copy are easier for your reader to follow. Consider how difficult it would be if you had to read the following listed information written out in a paragraph rather than set off in a *list*:

Service Parts List

SCHEMATIC REFERENCE NUMBER	PART NUMBER	COMPONENT DESCRIPTION
		Transistors and ICs
U101	20821	7805, Regulator
U102	352-27905	7905, Regulator
U103, 105, 106, 107, 108	50313	CA3140, Op-amp
U104	351-10339	LM339, Comparator
Q101	21048	D40D4 NPN Transistor

Q102, 103	30507	2N4124 NPN Transistor
		Zeners and SCRs
D101	50231	LM336, Regulator
D111, 112	35407	IN4742, 12V Zener
TR101	21516	2N5754, Triac

Source: Energy Concepts, Inc.

2.6.4 Use Illustrations Effectively

The old expression "a picture is worth a thousand words" is true, provided that the illustration says what it is meant to say. There are certain types of illustrations that are meant to do specific things. There are ten basic types of illustrations, although each has many variations. The ten basic types of illustrations are as follows:

- Line drawings
- Tables
- Pie charts
- Bar graphs
- Line graphs
- Flow charts and logic diagrams
- Schematics
- Photographs
- Cutaway diagrams
- Exploded diagrams

Line Drawings

A line drawing is an illustration or picture of something that has been rendered by an artist using only lines. Line drawings are common in technical writing. In fact, line drawings make up much of the illustrating in a number of types of graphics such as cutaway and exploded diagrams. Exhibit 2–4 shows line drawings of plenum-mounted humidifiers on two different types of furnace designs.

Exhibit 2–4
Line Drawings

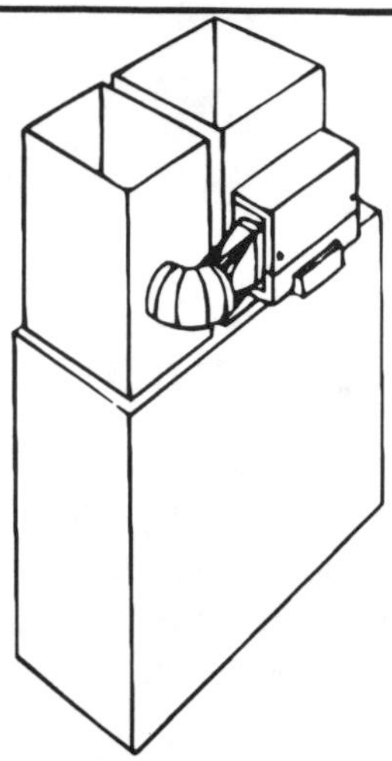

LOWBOY

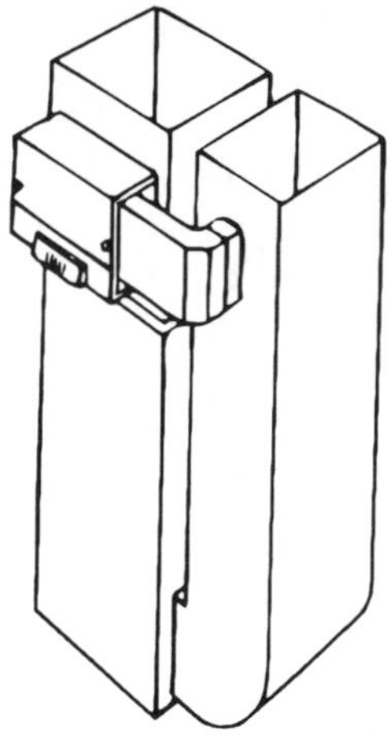

HIGHBOY

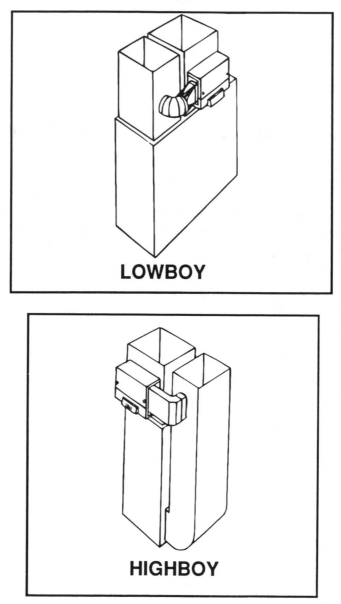

Source: Research Product Corporation.

Exhibit 2–5
Table

INPUT	TEST POINT A	TEST POINT B	TEST POINT C
(+) Full Scale .05, .5, 5, 50, and 500 V 50 μA, 50 mA, and 500 mA	50 mV	1.2 V	–1.2 V
(–) Full Scale .05, .5, 5, 50, and 500 V 50 μA, 50 mA, and 500 mA	–50 mV	–1.2 V	0
AC Full Scale .05, .5, 5, 50, and 500 V 50 μA, 50 mA, and 500 mA	42 mVAC	1.0 VAC	–.46 V
OHMS, Shorted Inputs	–50 mV approx.	–1.2 V approx.	n/a
LO OHMS, Shorted Input	–50 mV approx.	–1.2 V approx.	n/a

Source: Energy Concepts, Inc.

Tables

You should use tables to visually display a lot of information in one place (see Exhibit 2–5). Most of the time it is impossible to write clearly all the information within the body copy. The main advantages of using tables follow:

- Information is visually concise.
- Facts are easily compared.
- Quick references are easily done.
- Presentation of information is done more easily than in paragraph form.

Pie Charts

A pie chart is easy to draw and easy to interpret. A pie chart visually shows percentage relationships. Each "pie" is 100 percent of some-

Exhibit 2–6
Pie Chart

Barley Exports to Foreign Nations, 19××

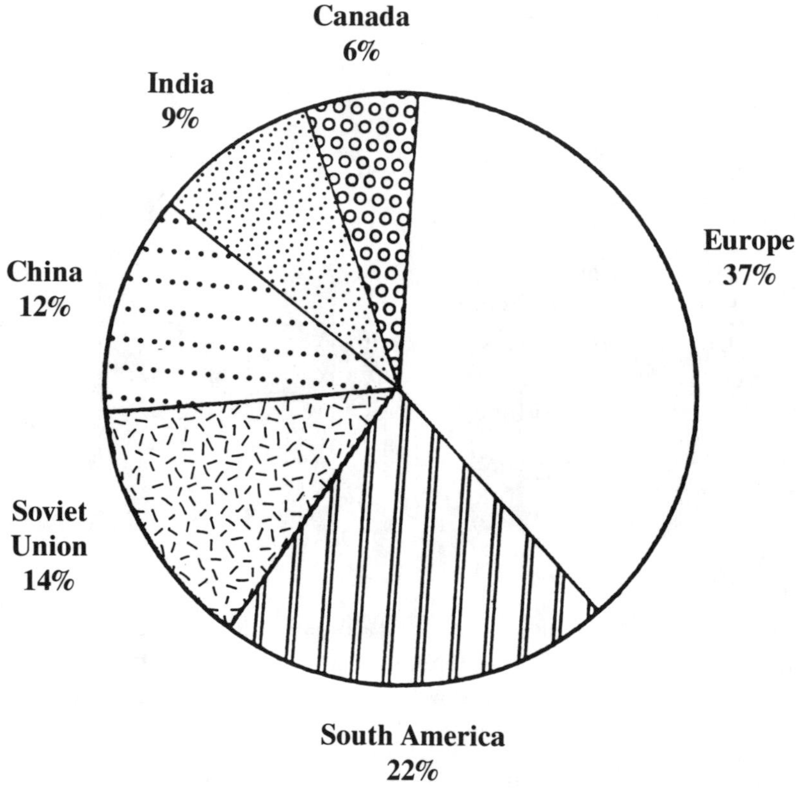

Source: *Handbook for Business Writing* by L. Sue Baugh, et al., National Textbook Co., 1993.

Exhibit 2–7
Bar Graph

Employee Distribution at Southland Electric Company, Inc.

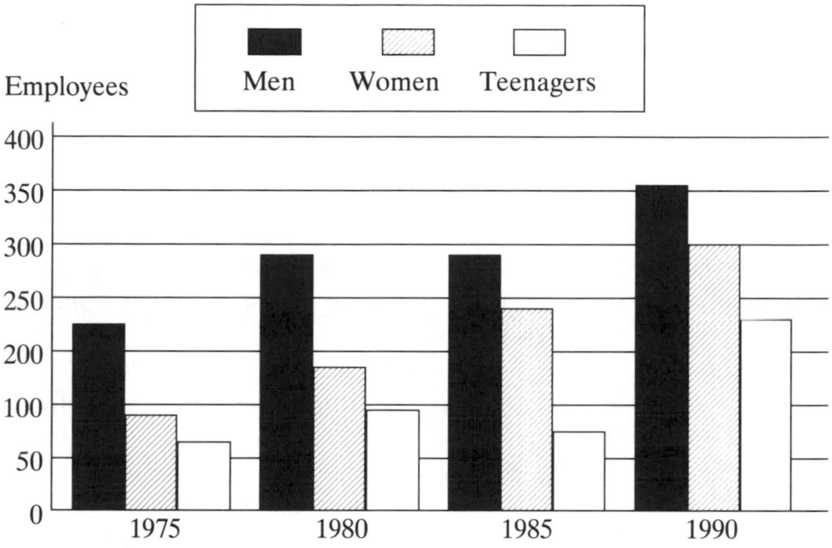

Source: *Handbook for Business Writing* by L. Sue Baugh, et al., National Textbook Co., 1993.

thing. Each section or "piece" is drawn to accurately represent a certain percentage of the whole pie. In this way you can actually show the percentage as well as discuss it in the copy. (See Exhibit 2–6.)

Bar Graphs

A bar graph shows individual quantities in terms of amount and time (see Exhibit 2–7). At one end of each "bar"' (showing its length) is the amount reference. At the other end of the bar is the time reference. You can draw a bar graph so that the bars run vertically or horizontally. The variation in bars should only be for length. Do not vary the width of the bars. Bar charts can also show trending, but only as a secondary purpose.

Line Graphs

The main purpose of a line graph is to show the trend between two variables (see Exhibit 2–8). You can plot a line graph from a bar graph by using the quantity of each bar as a point across the horizontal axis on the line graph. Another useful thing about a line graph is its ability to show comparisons of trends by plotting multiple lines. In Exhibit 2–8, you can see how the trend in resistance increases as airflow increases.

Flowcharts and Logic Diagrams

Flowcharts and logic diagrams show a process in various stages from beginning to end or the reverse. They can use a number of different symbols, from blocks to icons, depending on the need. The direction of flow should be absolutely clear and is usually indicated using arrows. You can also connect the blocks and then label the elements appropriately to show points of direction or use, such as in a wiring or hydraulics diagram. The flowchart in Exhibit 2–9 shows a flow of business for a warehouse operation that is tracked by computer software. The wiring diagram in Exhibit 2–10 shows where to make the connections and what they connect.

Schematics

Schematics show both process and layout of parts (see Exhibit 2–11). All schematics use symbols that are unique to the subject of the schematic. Therefore, be careful to consider your reader's ability to understand the symbols. A schematic's symbols and their meaning are like a foreign language. If your reader has not been trained in the specific discipline of the schematic (electronics, mechanics, or hydraulics, for example), he or she cannot understand anything about the illustration. When understood by your reader, schematics become an effective and comprehensive visual way to show process and spatial layout.

Exhibit 2–8
Line Graph

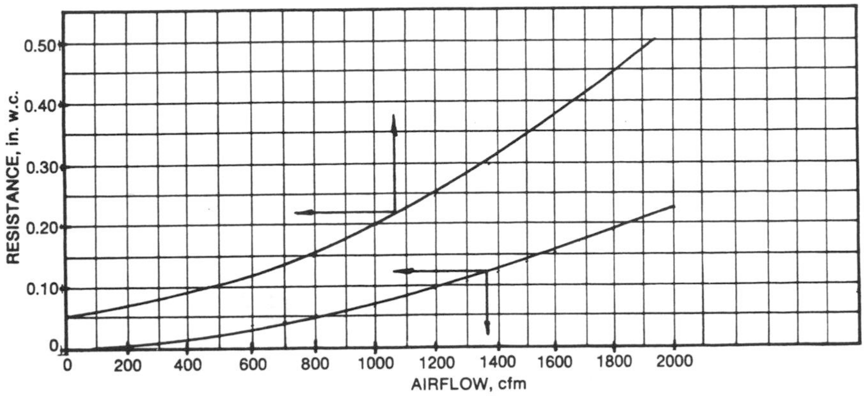

Source: Research Products Corporation.

Exhibit 2–9
Flowchart (partial)

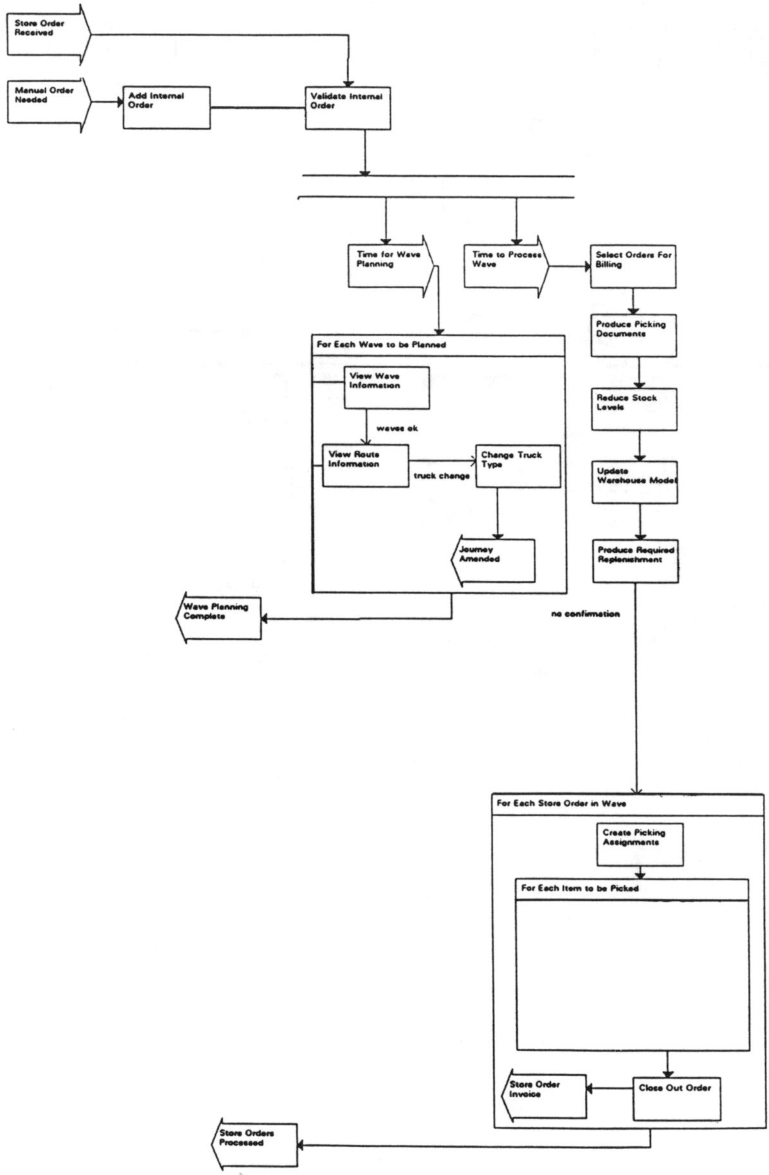

Source: BACG, Inc.

Exhibit 2–10
Logic Diagram

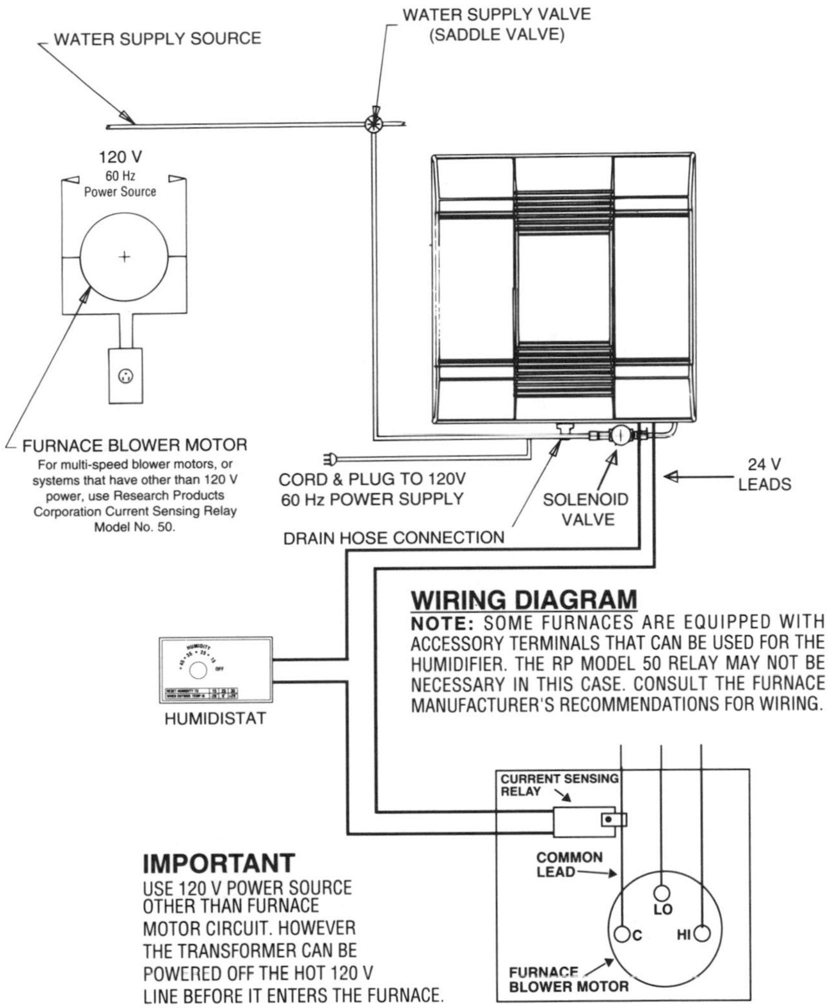

Source: Research Products Corporation.

Exhibit 2–11
Schematic (partial)

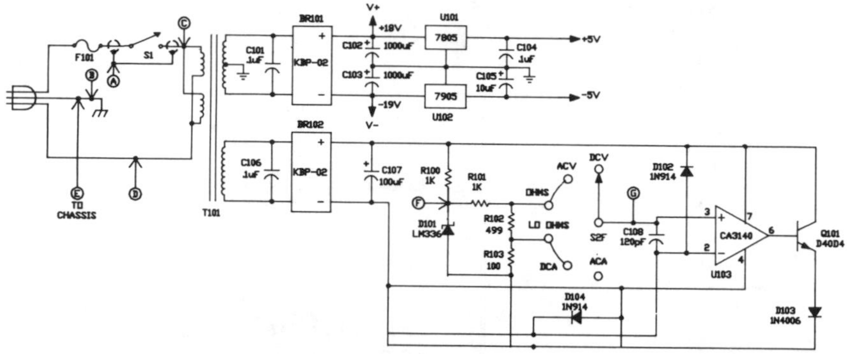

Source: Energy Concepts, Inc.

Exhibit 2–12
Photograph

Source: Research Products Corporation

Photographs

Photographs show absolute realism (Exhibit 2–12). When you need to show it absolutely as it looks, you would opt for a color photograph. Photographs work best when you want to show the shape or complete detail of an object or mechanism, such as a small motor. In contrast to this, a photograph showing absolute realism will do a poor job of showing a process where flow is involved. A photograph of hydraulic lines will not clearly show return lines. A drawing, however, can be colored or marked in such a way as to make the return lines obvious.

Cutaway Diagrams

A cutaway diagram shows what is inside of an enclosure. The illustration allows the reader to maintain a sense of the outside shape of

Exhibit 2–13
Cutaway Diagram

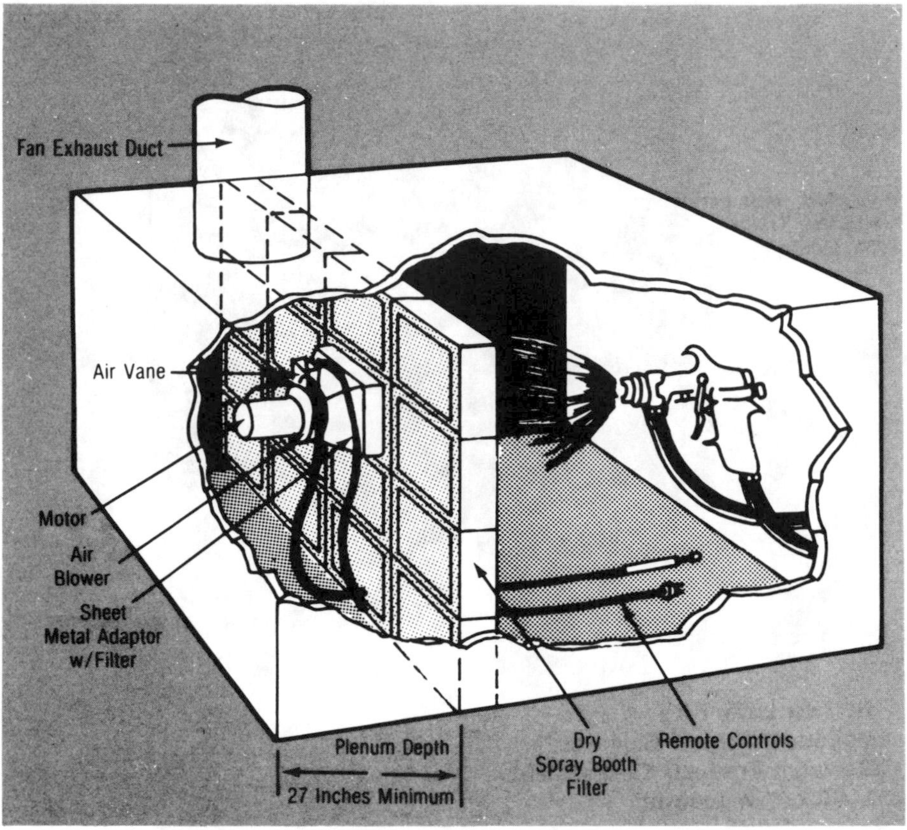

Source: Reprinted with permission, Copyright © 1984 Gardner Publications, Inc. and Jim Howery, Research Products Corporation.

the object while at the same time looking inside as though there was an opening cut into it. This type of drawing is especially useful in showing the inside of mechanisms and the inside of buildings and structures. The medical sciences have also used this type of illustration extensively to show students what is inside of the human body. Exhibit 2–13 shows the inside of an industrial spray paint booth in relation to its outside shape.

Exploded Diagrams

An exploded diagram shows the relationships of different physical elements that fit together (see Exhibit 2–14). Exploded diagrams deal exclusively with mechanisms and their respective parts. An exploded diagram is an excellent way to show how to assemble or disassemble a mechanism by showing the parts as though they were "exploding" in the exact position and connecting relationship to each other. You can use exploded drawings to great advantage in all assembly-type instructions.

2.6.5 Include Adequate Appendixes

Use an appendix at the end of a formal report or book to supplement or clarify. The information in an appendix is material that is pertinent to the body of writing but is either not critical or too voluminous to be placed in the main body of the text. Raw data, reinforcing information from tables, and supporting passages from other documents belong in an appendix when they are not critical to the text.

A document frequently contains more than one appendix. When this is the case, always number or label each appendix in the order that it relates to the text, and then refer to each one in the table of contents.

Exhibit 2–14
Exploded Diagram

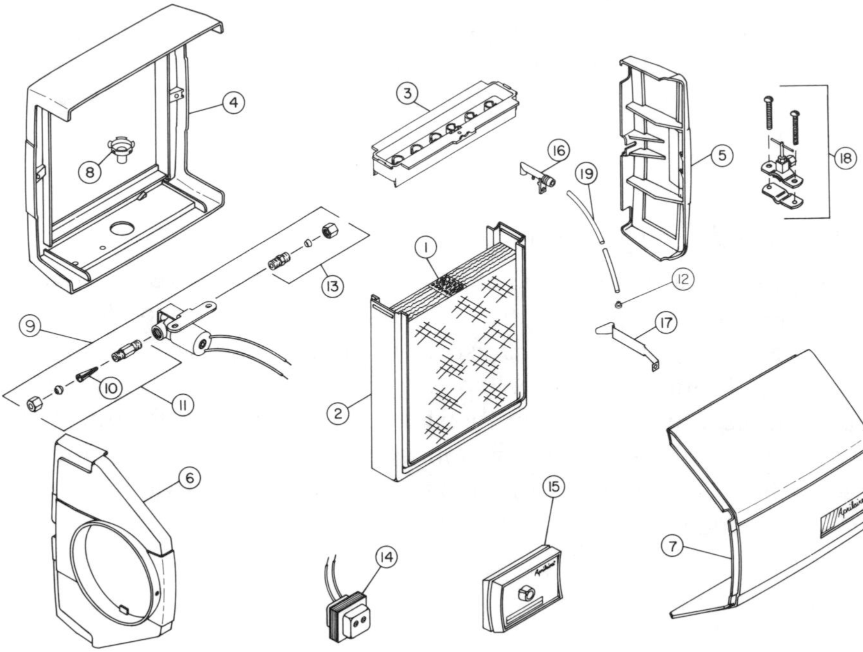

Instructions for Ordering Parts — Specify: MODEL NO. — PART NAME — PART NO.

NO.	PART NAME	QTY/CTN	**MODEL 550** PART NO.
1	Water Panel Evaporator	10	10
2	Scale Control Insert	10	4217
3	Water Distribution Tray	1	4218
4	Base	1	4219
5	End Panel	1	4220
6	Duct Panel	1	4221
7	Cover With Latch and Label	1	4222
8	Drain Spud	1	4223
9	Water Solenoid Valve (24 Volt)	1	4040
10	In Line Strainer	12	4004
11	Compression Fitting and Strainer	1	4102
12	Orifice (Yellow) .... (144/ctn.)	12 - 12 pks.	4231
13	Tube Fitting	6	4076
14	Transformer	1	4010
15	Humidistat	1	4016
16	Nozzle	1	4184
17	Cover Latch Spring	1	4225
18	Saddle Valve	1	4001
19	Feed Tube With Compression Sleeve	1	4226

Source: Research Products Corporation.

2.7 The Final Presentation

When you have gone to all the trouble involved in a well-written report, don't put a rubber band around it and toss it onto the reader's front door like the daily paper. It deserves better. You must present a report.

Formal reports should be bound in ring binders or covering folders that not only protect the report but also present an attractive appearance. Manuals should be bound professionally if they are to go to consumers and have wide circulation. Shorter and less formal reports should be clean and have a cover sheet on them. Never allow your final writing to be dirty or tattered. Always have your technical writing reflect a professional appearance, because it reflects on you and your efforts.

Writer's Workshop

1 Analyze the organization and development of a technical document in your field of expertise. Show the major points of the message and how they fit into the pattern of development. Are they parallel? What type of pattern was used?

2 Give examples of technical writing within your field of expertise that fit the following organizational patterns:
(a) general to specific;
(b) specific to general;
(c) chronological;
(d) sequential;
(e) cause and effect;
(f) comparison;
(g) spatial.

3 Choose a topic from your field of expertise that would fit into a 300–500 word informational document. Outline the document using the following outlining techniques:
(a) topic outline;
(b) sentence outline;
(c) paragraph outline.

Based on your subject, which was the most useful and why?

4 Give five examples of abstract words in your field of expertise. Convert the abstract words to concrete terms and concepts.

5 Give five examples of jargon within your field of expertise. How would you clarify each example to a reader who was not familiar with the meaning?

Self-Test Quiz

1 To determine the scope of a writing project, you must first determine the number of pages the document must be.

2 A far greater degree of definition is required for general readers than for technical readers.

3 A managerial reader is less concerned with technical detail than a technical reader.

4 You must identify your readers and classify them according to the two primary groups of either managerial or technical.

5 A report about a process in which you examine the whole process and then break it down into each of its consecutive steps is an example of *general to specific* development.

6 Chronological development is based on time.

7 The major problem with outlining is the time it adds to the writing assignment.

8 A topical outline tends to be the most complete type of outline.

9 Liberal use of topic heads tends to clutter the writing and confuse the reader.

10 Generous use of white space helps the reader organize the writing visually into readable portions.

Answer Key

1 F **2** T **3** T **4** F **5** T **6** T **7** F **8** F **9** F **10** T

Section 3

THE ELEMENTS OF TECHNICAL WRITING

3.1 Three Basic Elements of Form

Technical writing is perhaps the purest form of informational writing. It delivers factual information to an audience that must use that information for some specific purpose. In any type of technical writing, you will find one or a combination of three basic technical writing elements which are as follows:

1. Technical definitions
2. Technical descriptions
3. Technical instructions

These three elements of technical prose are found either by themselves or in combination with virtually all of the many forms of technical writing.

Rarely will all of the procedural steps be needed in any one definition, description, or set of instructions. The number of steps and procedures will vary with the nature of the audience. For instance, consider instructions meant for a professional HVAC installer who is going to install a central humidification system. This expert will not require a definition of humidity in the installation instructions. The expert will need, however, a comprehensive description of the physical dimensions of the unit and detailed instructions for its installation. By contrast, a student in a technical trade school will need comprehensive definitions as well as comprehensive descriptions in addition to the installation instructions.

3.1.1 Technical Definitions

Beyond all other types of informational writing, technical writing struggles with the effective and meaningful use of vocabulary. Much of technology is expressed through a specialized "language" of terms. Writers must learn this technical vocabulary, because it carries specific meaning only within a narrow field of technical knowledge. Therefore, many terms have no acceptable substitute in common language. Only one particular term will work within the context of the technical writing. Consequently, you must define these terms and concepts for the benefit of readers who might not have enough technical knowledge to understand them.

There are three basic approaches to defining technical terms and concepts:

1. Informal or parenthetical definitions
   A word or phrase in parentheses
   A word or phrase set off by commas
2. Formal or sentence definitions
   A definition that uses one or several sentences
   A definition based on three distinct elements.

   (1) The term itself

(2) The term's category
(3) The unique features of the term as compared with other terms or concepts in the category

3. Extended definitions
   Definitions extended through examples
   Definitions extended through analogy
   Definitions extended through analysis

Informal or Parenthetical Definitions

An informal definition is a brief explanation of a term written within the sentence that uses the term. The definition itself can be either a word or a short definitive phrase. Always use the most commonly understood and simplified term or phrase in the definition. Remember that an informal definition is not comprehensive but is instead a simple explanation. Set off the informal definition using either parentheses or commas. Following are some examples of informal or parenthetical definitions:

1. Tests showed that the myocardial infarction <u>(heart attack)</u> was severe enough to be fatal.
2. Ventricular fibrillation, <u>a random and irregular heartbeat</u>, is often the result of electric shock.
3. Because of the vacuum in a CRT <u>(cathode-ray tube)</u>, the CRT will implode, <u>break inward rather than outward</u>, if it is dropped or otherwise broken.
4. You may experience uncomfortable levels of humidity <u>(moisture contained in the air)</u> in a tropical climate.
5. You must periodically replace the brushes <u>(rotating brush-like conductive material)</u> in a power drill.
6. You must meter in <u>(regulate)</u> the hydraulic fluid entering the actuator.
7. This particular part uses a Woodruff Keyseat <u>(a type of standardized keyseat)</u>.
8. The angle of keenness <u>(an angle on the cutting tool that affects the strength of the tool)</u> must be considered when you make your tool selection for the job.

9. In this application, place insulators (materials that will not conduct electricity) at each of the corners of the configuration.
10. A time-delay relay (a relay capable of a number of timing functions) is called for in this application.

Formal or Sentence Definitions

A formal definition uses one or several complete sentences to define a term or concept. The formal definition uses three elements within a sentence to accomplish the definition.

1. The term or concept to be defined
2. The category of the term or concept
3. The uniqueness of the term or concept as contrasted with others in the category

The following are some examples of formal or sentence definitions:

Term: automatic control

Category: series of operations performed in a logical sequence

Uniqueness: without human intervention
An automatic control is a series of operations performed in a logical sequence without human intervention.

Term: electrical relay

Category: electromagnetic field that causes movement of an armature

Uniqueness: operates against spring tension to make or break electrical contacts
An electrical relay is an electromagnetic field that operates against spring tension to make or break electrical contacts.

Term: fittings

Category: connectors or closures

Uniqueness: for fluid power lines and passages
Fittings are connectors or closures for fluid power lines or closures.

Term: solenoid

Category: an electromagnetic field

Uniqueness: causes mechanical movement of a bar or plunger
A solenoid is an electromagnetic field that causes movement of a bar or plunger.

Term: time-delay relay

Category: a solid-state relay

Uniqueness: operates in many modes to provide a host of timing functions

A time-delay relay is a solid-state relay that operates in many modes to provide a host of timing functions.

Extended Definitions

You will often need more than a word, phrase, or sentence to define a term or concept. Under these circumstances, you will need to use an extended definition. An extended definition is an extension of a formal sentence definition into one or more paragraphs.

By extending the definition, you explore and discuss a number of the term's qualities and aspects. You may select from a variety of ways to extend definitions, depending on the complexity of your subject and the reader's technical level. In extended technical definition, the most common approach is through the use of one or more examples.

When you use specific examples, your reader is able to picture the various aspects and details of the term or concept you are defining. A specific example also brings an abstract idea into the everyday world of reality.

In the previous types of definitions, you have seen *time-delay relay* as a parenthetical and formal definition. The following example uses *time-delay relay* as an extended definition:

Time-Delay Relay

A time-delay relay is a solid-state relay that operates in many modes to provide a host of timing functions. You may sometimes need a delay in a hydraulic cycle. You can find examples of this type of delay in many kinds of machines.

In drilling and boring machines, you may need a delay after tool breakthrough to clean up the hole. In feed units, a delay is useful when a holding time is required during an operation. In die-casting machines, a delay may be required for the metal to cool after the shot and before ejection.

Another type of timing would be in step drilling, when the tool is advanced and retracted in steps to extract chips. A variety of timing devices are electric-motor driven types, thermal timers, pneumatic timers, and relay timers. The greatest variety of operating modes can now be found in solid-state delay timers. Some of these operations are delay on make, single shot, delay on break, and interval.

Source: Energy Concepts, Inc.

3.1.2 Technical Descriptions

Technical description can be either a part of a larger written work or it can be complete in itself. In most cases it will be a particular section of a larger work such as an operations manual or technical report.

Technical description is purely objective and factual. You can easily compare it with literary description, which primarily concerns itself with the reader's imagination and emotional reaction to the writing.

For example, if you were to read a technical description of the lift-off of a modern spacecraft, you would probably find exact acceleration figures in terms of foot-pounds of thrust and the time it takes to attain a certain altitude. It would also give you details of the acceleration in terms of Gs (the number of times greater the acceleration force exerted against the crew is than the force of gravity on earth). As you can see, the primary goal of this technical description would be to write in terms of facts and figures.

In contrast, consider a possible literary description of the same lift-off. It would instead concentrate on the "crushing force" against the pilot and the fears that the crew might experience as they are "blasted explosively into space." This description would concentrate on emotional experience more than objective facts and figures.

Technical description can be divided into two basic types: the description of a *technical mechanism* and the description of a *technical process*. A technical description of a mechanism can be about everything from new machines, devices used for measurement and analysis, to new equipment for purchase in the industrial or domestic environment. A technical description of a process can be about everything from processes that are controlled and manipulated by people to natural processes that may be virtually uncontrolled but nevertheless observed and monitored by people.

Mechanism Descriptions

The general structure of a mechanism description is made up of four main elements:

1. Define the mechanism.
   What is the main use of the mechanism?
   Where does the mechanism operate?
   When does the mechanism operate?

2. Explain the general operation.
   What are the major components?
   What pre-operational conditions are involved?
   To what extent is the mechanism humanly controlled?

3. Visually describe the mechanism as a whole.
   Give its general size and dimensions.
   Compare its shape to related mechanisms.

4. List and describe the component parts.
   List each specific part.
   How does the part function?
   Where does the part function?
   When does the part function?

An example is shown in Exhibit 3–1.

Step 1: Define the mechanism. *What is the main use of the mechanism?* This definition must take the mechanism as a whole and generally explain why it exists. Tell your reader how the mechanism is used in general and why the mechanism is needed. For example, a universal horizontal milling machine is a very complex mechanism with many specific uses. Its main use, however, is the cutting and altering of pieces of metal into tools and parts.

Where does the mechanism operate? The general location where a mechanism operates is often important to the definition. For instance, the rotating radar tracking system in an AWACS aircraft is located in the vertical dome on top of the aircraft. An enlarger is located in the darkroom area of a photo lab. These are locations that have been specialized for the use of the particular equipment that goes there.

When does the mechanism operate? The time interval or period that a mechanism operates is important to understanding it. The heat exchanger in a forced-air furnace does not operate until air temperature affects a thermostat that in turn energizes ignition in the exchanger. Another example might be a lighting system that is programmed to light at a specific time. The system activates because of a programmable controller set for that specific time.

Step 2: Explain the general operation. *What are the major components?* All mechanisms can be divided into several main parts. You need to tell your reader what these main divisions are in relation to the overall mechanism. For example, the wheels on an automobile are made up of hubs, wheels, brakes, and tires. In each of these divisions there are many more detailed parts.

What pre-operational conditions are involved? Sometimes there are conditions that must be met before the mechanism or machine can be operated. Some of these types of preconditions are temperature, humidity, or lighting. For example, specific types of lighting are a precondition for operating certain types of graphic arts equipment, such as a photostat machine.

To what extent is the mechanism humanly controlled? Mechanisms tend to be either directly or indirectly controlled by people. At the very least, the ability to initially start a mechanism is at someone's command. In other cases, less complex mechanisms are totally controlled and operated by people. For example, there is a great deal of control in the setup and operation of a manual lathe. There is much less control in the operation of a computerized lathe.

Some mechanisms operate other mechanisms but are indirectly controlled by people. These types of mechanisms are usually integral components of a larger overall mechansim or system of mechanisms that is ultimately controlled by people. For example, the carburetor on your car functions independently but is indirectly controlled by you at the gas pedal or throttle.

Step 3: Visually describe the mechanism as a whole. *Give its general size and dimensions.* Your basic visual description of a mechanism should give your reader a general sense of relative size and shape. Express these dimensions in units of measurement (or compare them to units of measurement) that are commonly understood. For instance, time in a nuclear reaction is measured in nanoseconds. A nanosecond is one-billionth of a second.

Compare its shape to related mechanisms. Comparisons to other, similar mechanisms may be helpful as well as some general contrasts. Keep the visual description simple and limit it to the mechanism as a whole. Remember that when you examine a mechanism, you notice the device in general before you take into account all of its details.

Step 4: List and describe the component parts. After you have described the general shape and functions of a mechanism, your readers will be ready for a detailed description of each of its main functioning parts. This description is much the same as describing the mechanism as a whole.

List each specific part. Define each part and explain its general use as it relates to the whole mechanism. In order to approach each of these parts, you must follow a logical sequence in terms of operation or location.

How does the part function? Each part will have a specific function and reason to exist. Give this function and its relationship to the mechanism as a whole. For example, valve springs have a very specific function and reason for being as they relate to the overall mechanism of a four-stroke internal combustion engine. They close the valves at the end of the intake or exhaust stroke of the engine.

Where does the part function? At times the position of the part may not be obvious and may need comment. For example, the lens-barrel release on a particular brand of camera is directly on the left side of the lens barrel at the front of the camera. Illustrations are invaluable when it comes to showing where individual parts and components are located. The reader can literally see where the part is located in order to operate or otherwise manipulate the part.

Exhibit 3–1
Mechanism Description (partial)

1. General definition

GENERAL
The Energy Concepts Digital Multimeter is an easily operated, versatile instrument for students and technicians in all laboratory applications. The unit is self-contained, line operated, and features advanced solid-state design.

2. General operation

The electrical quantities being measured are read from the 3 1/2-digit Digital Display on the front panel. You can measure six separate functions, with each function having several different ranges. You will use the CURRENT section of the multimeter to make current measurements. Use the VOLTS/OHMS section for voltage and resistance measurements. You may select the function by pressing one of the six blue pushbuttons between the range switches. Press only one of these switches at any given time.

3. Visual description

FRONT PANEL CONTROLS
The following paragraphs contain a description of each control and receptacle. The descriptions are keyed to the encircled numbers in Figure 1-1, which is a front view of the Digital Multimeter.

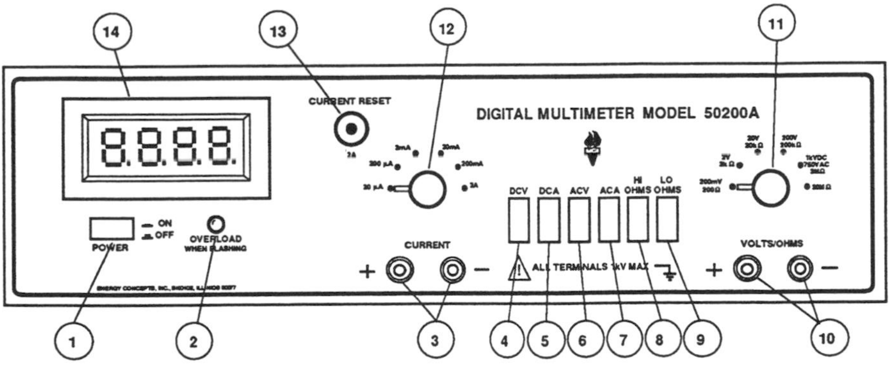

POWER SWITCH
Use this red pushbutton switch to apply power from the AC line to the unit. Press the switch to the in position to turn it ON. Then press it to the out position to turn it OFF.

4. List and description of component parts

* * *

DIGITAL DISPLAY
This 3 1/2 digit Digital Display shows numbers from 000 to 1999. When you select a range, the decimal point shifts as required. When you apply a negative voltage, a negative sign precedes the number. On the other hand, the number is positive when no sign precedes the number. No polarity sign will show for AC or resistance readings.

PREPARATION FOR USE
The energy Concepts Digital Multimeter is portable. It can be placed on any flat, vibration-free surface for satisfactory operation. The Digital Multimeter operates in a closed case, so venting is not necessary. However, space at the front of the instrument should permit electrical connections to the input terminals and changing modes of operation.

Pre-operational conditions

The operator should understand thoroughly the functions of all the controls, terminals, and indicators before proceeding with the meter setup and operation.

Place the instrument in the desired operating location. Then connect the AC power cable to an appropriate 50/60 Hz source. The input power is normally for 120 VAC unless 230 VAC is specifically requested.

Source: Energy Concepts Inc.

When does the part function? Not all parts function at the same time. Some are activated at different times, such as the keys on a computer keyboard. Sometimes parts and components only operate under rare circumstances, such as the safety airbags on a car that inflate during a collision. Other parts operate and function all the time, as in the case of electrical metering devices for electricity and water.

Process Descriptions

Some processes, such as performing a software routine on a computer, are done in part or totally by people. Other processes are totally uncontrolled by people, such as the movement of the planets or weather patterns. Some processes, such as detonating an explosive device, are performed completely by machines, but starting the process can be controlled by people. This partial control is usually a matter of starting or stopping a process. But whether controlled or uncontrolled, you need to clarify exactly what the process is and what it is not before you attempt to describe it.

A process is dynamic. It has action and change across time. These elements of action, change, and time are always present to one degree or another, and they must be clear to your reader in your description.

Process description is not instruction. In a process description, your goal is to have your reader understand the process. With instructions, you want your reader not only to understand the process but also to perform the process.

There are many times when understanding the process is necessary but performing it is not necessary. For example, a description of a certain type of surgery will be necessary for an administrator to buy the necessary equipment for the hospital. It would not be necessary, however, for the administrator to be able to perform that operation in order to make the purchasing decision.

The general structure of a technical description of a process is made up of three main steps:

1. Define the process.
   Why does the process take place?
   When does the process take place?
   Where does the process take place?
   Who or what performs the process?

2. Describe the process as a whole.
   What are the major divisions of the process?
   What materials are necessary?
   What special skills are required?
   What pre-process conditions are involved?
   What are the time requirements?

3. List and describe each step.
   List and describe the specific step.
   Why does this step take place?
   Where does this step take place?
   How much time does the step take?

An example is shown in Exhibit 3–2.

Step 1: Define the process. *Why does the process take place?* The answers to this question will vary depending on the process itself. The process of a "hand-off" from one cell to another in cellular communications takes place because people want continued transmission and reception on a mobile phone. The process of tuning an automobile engine takes place to ensure efficient and effective performance of the engine.

When does the process take place? Some natural processes take place only under certain circumstances and may not be predictable. Others, such as cell growth, are ongoing. A process that is under the control of people is usually predictable and has conditions under which it will take place.

Where does the process take place? The answer will often be obvious, as in the case of an operating room or a photographic darkroom. At other times, the location is not obvious but is at the heart of understanding the process, such as the switching process that is involved with the transmission of a call from a land-line to a cellular phone receiver.

Who or what performs the process? Some processes are performed by people and/or machines. Sometimes they occur but are not performed. The purpose of the description and the technical needs of your reader will determine the depth of description here. For instance, just about anyone can take their body temperature or heart rate, but only a medical doctor who is a qualified surgeon can perform surgery. Just about anyone can change a tire on their car, but only a qualified brake specialist can replace or adjust a car's braking system.

Step 2: Describe the process as a whole. *What are the major divisions of the process?* Processes tend to have major divisional elements that group together the individual steps in the process. For instance, there are four major divisions in the process of making a black-and-white photographic print. These four main divisions are *enlargement, chemical processing, washing,* and *drying*. In each of these divisions, there are a number of individual steps needed to complete that major divisional element. Always present the major divisions of the process in their correct order of occurrence.

What materials are necessary? Natural processes will not require any materials, but you may need special materials to observe them, such as microscopes or telescopes. On the other hand, if the process is controlled by people, a great deal of special materials and equipment may be needed. This is most evident when describing a procedure that will require the purchase of equipment. Diagnostic testing always requires test equipment. You may often need not only to list the needed materials and equipment but also to describe the equipment.

What special skills are required? Any time people perform the process, skill of some sort is required. This element becomes critical when special skill or training is required. For instance, the process of putting fuel into your car basically requires knowing how to operate the fuel pump and where to put the nozzle. On the other hand, the process of adjusting the carburetion system on a competition dragster requires specialized knowledge and training. Always clearly tell your reader what the required skills are and the extent of experience and knowledge necessary for the process. This section does not always require a great deal of coverage, but it must be addressed for your reader.

What pre-process conditions are involved? Some processes depend on certain temperatures, ventilation, or lighting conditions before the process can occur. The example of the photographic process mentioned earlier depends on darkness or "safe lighting" during much of the process. This condition must be present before the process can take place.

What are the time requirements? Time always plays a role in describing the process as a whole. Remember that the process is not only the actions involved but also how they relate to time. The process of intake, compression, ignition, and exhaust in an internal combustion engine takes a certain amount of time. It is slow if you compare it to nuclear fission. It is fast, however, if you compare it to the decomposition of lead-based paint. Describing time is most effectively approached through comparison and contrast. In order to effectively describe the time element of a process, describe the process in time measurements such as hours, minutes, or seconds. Then make a comparison to a process familiar to your reader in order to give meaning to the process time.

Step 3: List and describe each step. *List and describe the specific step*. Specifically state the step in terms of the action taking place. Start with the first step and list it as such. The listing of each successive step in sequence shows your reader when one step ended and the next began.

Why does this step take place? Tell your reader what is actually done or accomplished with each step. By telling your reader what is accomplished by the action, you give meaning to the individual step.

Where does this step take place? In many cases, where the step takes place will be obvious to your reader and will not warrant a reference. In other instances, a reference to the location of a specific action may be critical to understanding the process. An example might be to specify which valve opens on the intake step.

How much time does the step take? Just as any overall process has a time element that the reader must understand, each individual step also has a time reference. In some processes, the reference to overall time may be sufficient and the time involved in an individual step may not be necessary to mention. In other cases, where the time of each step varies and those times are critical to the outcome of the process, they must be emphasized. For instance, the time involved for the chemical development step has a critical time element and is much longer than the stop bath step that immediately follows during film development. (See Exhibit 3–2.)

3.1.3 Technical Instructions

Technical instructions have much in common with technical descriptions, with one great difference. Instructions must assist the reader in successfully performing the process as well as in understanding it. This need for the reader to perform the process correctly places a greater burden of comprehension on both the writer and the reader. If the process is not performed correctly, people can be harmed or equipment ruined.

Exhibit 3–2
Process Description

"Asphalt Plants Solving Old Problems"

No one has worked harder than asphalt plant manufacturers to develop new technology to overcome old problems. As a result, today's asphalt plant bears little resemblance to the plant of 25 years ago. Although the traditional batch plant is still popular for its ability to produce a high-quality mix and vary the mix specifications, the drum mixer has clearly captured the market: Today virtually every new asphalt plant sold is a drum mix plant.

The drum mix plant is highly productive and efficient, and it can be designed to be easily transported. Early concerns over the quality of the mix produced by drum mixers have been laid to rest. Today's plants produce a mix equal to or better than mixes produced by batch plants.

Process definition

The first drum mixers, introduced around 1970, were parallel-flow design. Later, counter-flow plants were developed. Although the design of drum mixers has evolved over the years to deal with situations such as emissions, control requirements, mix quality, use of recycled product, and efficient operations, parallel-flow and counter-flow are still the two basic types of drum mixers, and each has advantages and disadvantages.

General process definition

In the parallel-flow plant, aggregate is introduced at the same end of the drum as the flame. Counter-flow plants introduce the aggregate at the opposite end, away from the flame.

Parallel-flow plants have the advantage of providing both radiant and conductive energy to reclaimed asphalt product, or RAP. Further, a large amount of the dust generated in the production process is captured by the asphalt, preventing it from being discharged into the air. The high temperatures of the

Detailed process description

gas stream, however, tend to turn the moisture and oils in the virgin materials and RAP into smoke.

The counter-flow system's design allows the virgin and RAP to be introduced outside of the combustion gases, reducing the amount of smoke created. Smoke is also consumed by the burner. With its lower smoke levels, the counter-flow system is particularly popular in areas that restrict or prohibit visible smoke from being released. While a counter-flow system emits less smoke than parallel-flow system, it also applies less heat energy to the RAP, making it less efficient at higher production rates with higher ratios of RAP.

Source: Lynn Lanberg, *Construction Equipment Magazine*.

Technical instructions are usually a matter of performing some physical process. This can include such typical actions as assembling, operating, maintaining, inspecting, repairing, or testing. All these activities have the people element in common. In any of these activities, the person performing them must not only understand the process but also must do it correctly.

The most common form of written technical instruction is an instruction manual. These manuals may be for general use and operation of a piece of equipment, or they may have a far more specific use, such as testing procedures or maintenance procedures.

The general structure of technical directions, whether as a part of a larger written work or standing alone, consists of three main steps:

1. Give the purpose for the instructions.
   Why do you perform the instructions?
   When do you perform the instructions?
   Where do you perform the instructions?

2. List all conditions that must be met prior to performance.
   What are the safety considerations?
   What are the environmental considerations (location, temperature, light, ventilation, etc.)?
   List all needed equipment and materials.
   What are the time constraints?

3. Give the actual sequence of instructions.
   List each instructional step in sequence.
   Write each instruction in the imperative mood.
   Write each step with the "you attitude."
   Give brief descriptions as needed in side notes.
   Use visuals to help your reader see the action.

Step 1: Give the purpose for the instructions.

Give a brief description of the process and define the purpose of its overall function. The depth of your description and definition of the instructions will depend on your reader and the scope of the instructions themselves. In many cases, such as full operational manuals, a formal process description will appear in the manual before the instructions themselves.

Step 2: List all conditions that must be met prior to performance.

These conditions will include such things as the following:

- equipment required
- special skills required
- temperature, humidity, and lighting specifications
- time restraints

Step 3: Give the actual sequence of instructions.

Number the list of instructions in the order that they are performed. At times, you will need to combine brief description and clarification. The use of visuals will greatly help your reader to see the correct action to take in each instruction. Along with visuals, use side notes to clarify certain actions or warn the reader about others.

Each step must be written in the imperative mood. The subject "you" will usually be unstated. In other instances, you may find it

Exhibit 3–3
General Audience Technical Instructions (partial)

Experiment Objectives

Purpose for instruction

Upon successful completion of this experiment, you should be able to figure the IMA for a gear train and a worm gear system for gear teeth numbers.

Equipment Required

List conditions prior to instruction

- Support Stand Set (following parts)
  - Mechanical Breadboard
  - Two Support Rods with Base
- Spur Gear with Bracket
- Worm Gear
- Two Small Weight Hangers
- Small Slotted Weight Set
- 30 cm Ruler
- Nylon Cord

Introduction

A **gear** is a wheel with teeth that is connected to an axle. When these teeth mesh with the teeth of a gear of different size, a mechanical advantage can be obtained. The gear to which the input force is applied in a pair of gears is called the *input gear*. The gear receiving the force from the input gear is the *output gear*.

Procedure

Detailed sequence of instructions

Refer to the detailed figures that follow when assembling your equipment.

1. Mount the support rods on the breadboard.
2. Mount the spur gear bracket near the top of the support rods.
3. Tie a 30 cm length of cord to each of the spindles. Pass the string through the hole in the spindle, and knot the end. Tie the other end of both strings to a weight hanger. See Figure 1.

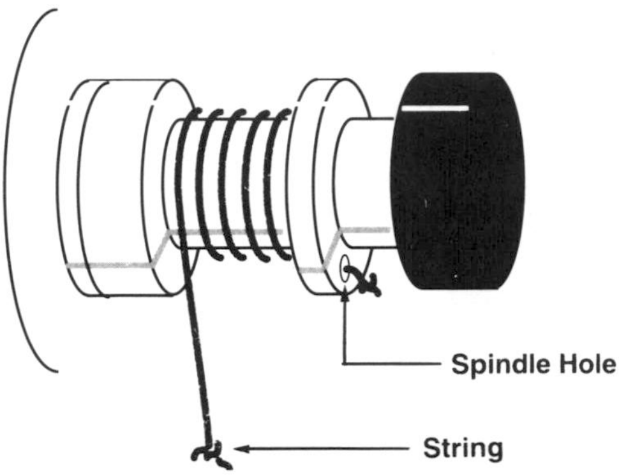

Figure 1
Attaching strings to spindles

4. Refer to Figure 2 for the proper gear designations.

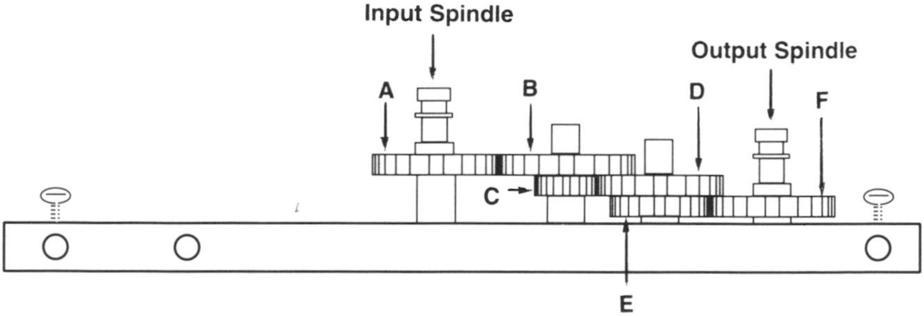

Figure 2
Gear designations

5. Tighten the output string by turning the output spindle. Place the output hanger on the breadboard directly below the output spindle.
6. Wind the input string around the input spindle. Do this until the weight hanger is suspended about 3 cm below the bracket. See Figure 3.

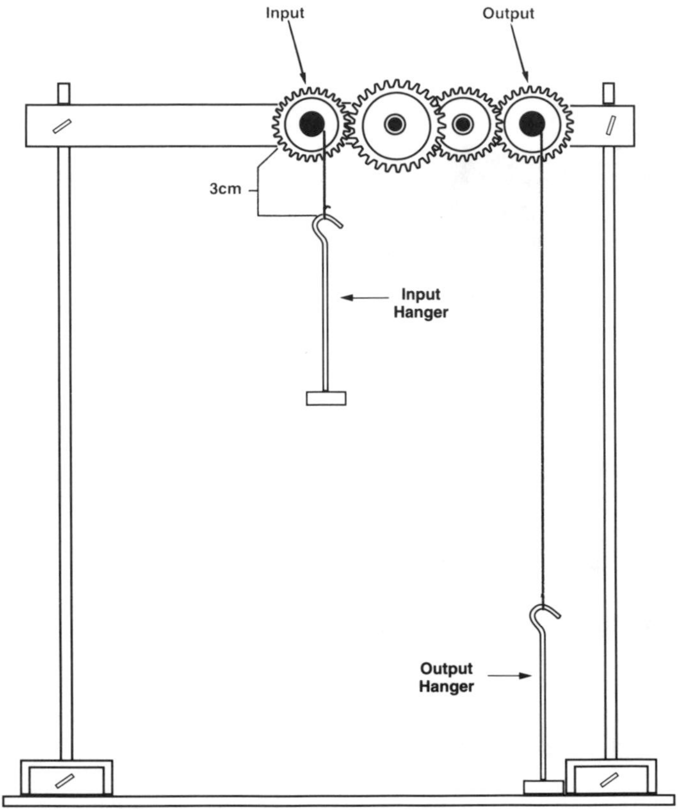

Figure 3
Weight hanger placement

effective to actually use the pronoun "you" as the imperative subject. This is the only acceptable style for writing technical instructions. The old-fashioned impersonal and third-person passive style of writing is totally ineffective in technical instructions.

Exhibits 3–3 and 3–4 reflect the different audiences technical writers must be able to address: general and technical.

In Exhibit 3–3, the instructions are for a student in a technical trade school. Students are at the general audience level in readership. As is evident in these instructions, they encompass the entire set of steps for definition and description.

In Exhibit 3–4, the instructions are for a technician who installs HVAC equipment. The technician does not need a great deal of definition and background due to technical expertise and experience.

Exhibit 3–4

Professional/Expert Technical Instructions (partial)

Aprilaire® HUMIDIFIER MODEL 110

BEFORE BEGINNING INSTALLATION, SEE OPTIONAL INSTALLATIONS ON REVERSE SIDE.

1 Draw a level horizontal line on the warm air plenum for positioning the bottom edge of this template. Be sure there is at least 2½″ above the furance jacket for drain line clearance. Mark the four corners of the opening to be cut by tracing around the radius of the four cutouts in the template. Mark the two (2) 7/64″ dia. holes. These must be accurate. Remove template and retain for reference.

Using a straight edge, mark the opening to be cut from the plenum by connecting the four corners. Drill two (2) 7/64″ holes.

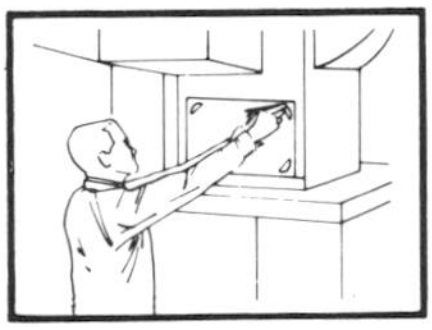

2 Cut plenum opening.

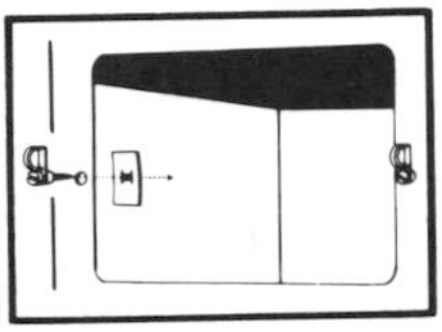

3 Attach two swing locks, using the tinnerman clips provided.

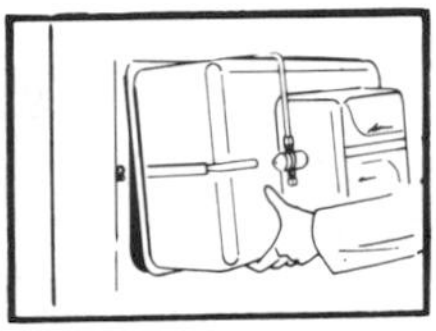

4 Position unit between swing locks. Push unit up and engage molded "U" Channel with the sheet metal at top of opening. Push unit in at bottom and slide down so the molded "U" Channel engages with sheet metal at bottom of opening.

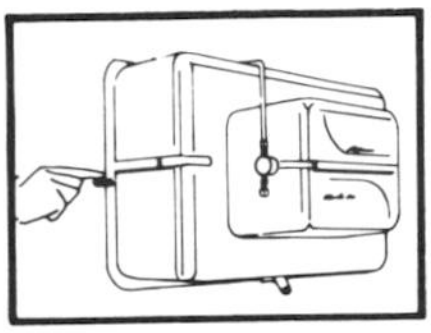

5 Turn swing locks to secure unit to plenum.

Writer's Workshop

1 Compose ten sentences using acronyms and technical terms common to your field of expertise. Define each acronym within each sentence using a parenthetical definition.

2 Compose ten sentence definitions using the terms from the previous exercise.

3 Define a concept or term common to your field of expertise using an extended definition. Depending on the subject, include a simple sketch, diagram, or schematic.

4 Write a description of a mechanism or process common to your field of expertise. Direct the description to a general reader. Be sure to use all areas in the text directions appropriate to the subject and reader. If this had been directed to a managerial or technical reader, how would it differ from a description intended for a general reader?

5 Write instructions for one or more of the following:
(a) loading a 35mm camera;
(b) installing an automatic garage door opener;
(c) putting up curtain rods;
(d) changing a tire on a car;
(e) fixing a paper jam in the copier;
(f) installing, fixing, or performing maintenance in an area common to your field of expertise.

Write the instructions for a person with relatively low technical understanding of the subject in general. How would these instructions differ if written to a person with a thorough understanding of the subject?

Self-Test Quiz

1 An informal definition uses only a single word or phrase.

2 An extended definition makes use of visuals.

3 A mechanism description first lists and describes the mechanism's parts and then explains its general operation.

4 A process description is concerned only with processes that require some degree of human control.

5 Technical instructions always deal with human control or intervention.

Answer Key

1 T **2** T **3** F **4** F **5** T

Section 4

FORMS OF TECHNICAL WRITING I: Memo Reports and Formal Reports

4.1 The Five Basic Forms of Technical Writing

In technical writing you will find many variations of reports and documents that are classified as technical writing. All of these variations and forms of technical writing can be divided into five basic types, or forms, of technical writing.

The five basic forms of technical writing are as follows:

- Technical Memo Reports
- Technical Formal Reports
- Technical Proposals (Section 5)

- Technical Manuals (Section 5)
- Technical Articles (Section 5)

In each of these five forms, you will see procedural steps on how to write each of them. Rarely will all of the procedural steps be needed in any one piece of technical writing. The number of steps and procedures will vary with the nature of the audience.

4.2 The Memo Report

The memo report is the most common and prevalent type of technical writing found in industry today. It is an informal report and is strictly an internal type of communication. It is called a memo report because the word *memo* is derived from the word *memorandum*. A memo report is not a long report. It deals primarily with brief internal communication that ranges from several paragraphs to several pages. The key to writing effective memo reports is brevity and simplicity. The typical memo report is made up of the following parts:

1. Heading information
2. Statement of purpose
3. Background statement
4. Discussion
5. Conclusions
6. Recommendations

4.2.1 Heading Information

Heading information gives the reader the writing solution. It specifically tells your reader the date of the memo report. This date is crucial to keeping files. It tells to whom the memo is being written. This is usually a single reader, but it also may be a group or a number of individuals. The heading information tells the reader who wrote the memo report. This again can be either a single person or a group. And finally, heading information gives the subject of the report.

Heading information is made up of four basic topic headings, as follows:

1. Date: ______________________________
2. To: ______________________________
3. From: ______________________________
4. Subject: ______________________________

The order of these topics is not important, but all four topics must be included in the heading.

Sometimes the receiver of the memo report is a single person, but photocopies are distributed to others who are less directly involved in the matter at hand. The names of individuals who receive copies are noted in the heading information after the abbreviation "cc:" (for "carbon copy").

4.2.2 Statement of Purpose

The statement of purpose tells the reader why the memo report has been written. Effective statements of purpose are always direct and concise. They sacrifice subtlety for directness.

4.2.3 Background Statement

A background statement should be brief and concise. It provides the reader with an overview of the events and circumstances that have led to the report. It also allows a recap and reminder for the reader who refers to the memo report at a later date.

4.2.4 Discussion

The discussion is the objective and factual written communication of your technical message. It is a detailed and complete message about the subject. The discussion is where the basic organizational pattern and outline of your ideas are put into written form.

4.2.5 Conclusions

Conclusions are the reasons or causes of technical conditions and situations. These are your findings or results about whatever it is that you are writing.

4.2.6 Recommendations

Recommendations are your suggestions based on your conclusions. They are your professional opinions about what should be done.

4.3 Typical Memo Reports

The types of informal, memo-style reports are by no means limited to the examples in this section. Although informal reports come in many structures, they all follow the memo style of headings. Remember to communicate the message in a way that is quickly and easily understood. In this way, action on the report can also take place promptly and easily. These basic types of informal reports can serve as models for your own report needs as they arise. These basic types are as follows:

- Feasibility reports
- Inside proposals
- Status/progress reports
- Test reports
- Trip reports
- Trouble reports

4.3.1 Feasibility Reports

The purpose of a feasibility report is to show whether undertaking a certain project or path of action will have success or failure. The likelihood of success must be weighed against the odds for failure. The report presents the evidence for that set of odds for or against the success of the project.

The structure of this type of report is as follows:

1. Memo-report headings
2. Purpose
3. Background
   —Procedures and methods
   —Alternatives
4. Discussion
5. Conclusions
6. Recommendations

Feasibility Report

Date: ____________________

To: ____________________

From: ____________________

Subject: *Should motor-driven linear actuators replace double-acting hydraulic cylinders on pinch rollers?*

Purpose:
The purpose of this report is to study the feasibility of having motor-driven linear actuators (ball-screw style) replace the double-acting hydraulic cylinders on the pressure-heated pinch rollers for the 24" counter-top laminator. Feasibility is based on economic and work-effectiveness factors.

Background:
About 22 years ago, Acme purchased the Otto 24" laminator currently being used at the Melville plant.

This machine uses three sets of hydraulic cylinders (2 per pinch roll) to exert 800 psi as the laminated top exits the gluer and enters the press area.

Depending on what size thickness the overall top will measure (1/4", 3/8", 1/2", 3/4"), you must manually adjust the clevis end of these cylinders.

This results in a set-up time of about 90 minutes. Operator controls for the pinch rollers are "full-extend" or "full-extract" with no middle settings.

Leaks in this existing system are a constant problem. The petroleum based oil attacks the glue that holds the laminate to the base wood.

Discussion:
Current technology in laminating machines uses motor-driven ball-screw actuators in place of hydraulic cylinders. These motors use a closed-loop feedback system that allows for PLC (programmable logic controller) based control. Consequently,

set-up time decreases from 90 minutes to 5 minutes. Because these actuators are motor driven, we can completely eliminate the hydraulic system.

The estimated cost to remove the existing hydraulic system and install the new motor-driven actuators has the following breakdown:

Motor actuators & controllers	$265,500.00
Removal & installation labor	$93,300.00
PLC operator training	$7,500.00
First-year cost	$366,300.00

The 24" counter-top laminator currently produces $4.4 million of product in 2,000 hours of operation at a production rate-per-minute of $35.67. This is based on using the figure of 85 minutes of saved set-up time and an average of 7.5 set-ups per week on a 50-week production schedule.

The projected increases in production are as follows:

Annual set-ups:	375 (50 × 7.5)
Total minutes saved	31,875 (375 × 85)
Increased production	$1,136,981.20 ($35.67 × 31,875)
Additional set-up adjustment factor	0.94
Adjusted increased production	$1,068,762.30 ($1,136,981 × 0.94)

Conclusions:
An investment of $366,300.00 of new motor-driven actuators will increase production at a rate of $1,068,762.30. This equates to a payback period of 17.2 weeks. Assuming both systems require the same amount of maintenance time, additional savings will result from less product damage from hydraulic leaks (estimated at $87,000.00). Another additional feature is the ability of the Otto laminator to run short orders (less than 100 pcs) because of reduced set-up time.

Recommendations:
The motor-driven linear actuators should be purchased and installed as soon as possible.

Courtesy: Larry Mielcarz, Consultant.

4.3.2 Inside Proposals

An inside proposal is a reporting document that stays inside the firm. It is usually prepared by a single person or department and submitted to a single person of higher authority for approval. Its purpose is to persuade the reader to allow or follow a particular plan or course of action. This usually entails the capital expenditure for equipment or personnel. It could be for such things as a new piece of plant or office equipment or for the authorization to hire additional expertise in manpower.

The structure of this type of report is as follows:

1. Memo-report headings
2. Background
3. Proposal
4. Cost breakdown
5. Proposed schedule

Proposal

Date: ____________________

To: ____________________, General Sales Mgr.

From: ____________________, Sales Engineer

Subject: *Hand-held tachometers for field sales engineers*

Background:
For the past year it has become apparent that our field sales engineers would greatly benefit from having hand-held tachometers to measure rotational shaft speed and linear line speed.

Over the past year, I have had no fewer than 16 instances where I have had to rely on a customer's word or his "best guess" about the speed of a motor, conveyor, or other mechnical device. Even nameplate data are questionable, especially on older equipment, because of years of machine modifications. In most of these cases, materials were returned because incorrect speed data were used to calculate gearbox and variable frequency drive sizes. As a result, customer projects were required to be held up while correct speed readings could be taken and the correct material shipped.

Proposal:
I propose that each of the six field sales engineers be issued a model #610 electronic hand-held tachometer with carrying case.

Cost Breakdown:
If each sales engineer averages 16 returns (this is a conservative estimate based on experience) because of speed miscalculations, the field will generate 96 RGRs (Return Goods Requests). We know from internal audits that each RGR is presently averaging $45.00. A model #610 tachometer lists at $375.00 each. We would need six of them. Consider the following breakdown in costing:

Six model #610 tachometers (6 × $375.00) $2,250.00

Cost of RGRs (96 × $45.00) $4,320.00

This is an initial savings over the first year after purchase of $2,070.00:

$4,320.00 – $2,250.00 .... $2,070.00

Suggested Time Frame:
Since all of the sales engineers will be in for the corporate office meeting during the second week of September, this would be a good time to give each sales engineer a tachometer and schedule them for a one-hour training session with the tachometers.

Courtesy: Larry Mielcarz, Consultant.

4.3.3 Status/Progress Reports

Periodic reports, sometimes called activity reports, allow management to stay informed on staff progress with ongoing technical work and projects. The most common types of periodic reports are weekly, monthly, and quarterly reports. Remember that these reports are primarily to keep management informed on technical work in progress. Because the report will contain information about ongoing work familiar to all concerned, there is no need for purpose, conclusions, or recommendations sections. The structure of the report tends to be abbreviated, as follows:

- Memo-report headings
- Status of projects

Status Report

Date: __________________

To: __________________

From: __________________

Subject: *Status report for week of X/X/19XX—*
Plastic retainer for #622 bearing

R&D received the final CAD drawings. The corporate legal department has filed the preliminary paperwork for patent protection. Final cost for the extrusion dies amounted to $125,000.00. Production should begin in early January.

Hydro-seal for #622 bearing:
Early tests show that the ethylene propylene seal developed serious leakage problems at rotational speed over 4000 RPM. Additional tests are scheduled for next week.

Pump-Master inner race:
Six additional field reports arrived this week, bringing the total to 88 reports. These reports are on the chromium plating on the Pump-Master inner race and its flaking and blistering at

high temperature (100 C to 120 C). All the reports are limited to those inner races with 2.00" bores or less. Plating U.S.A. (our subcontractor) has been notified and batch numbers have been submitted.

New roller bearing #1221:
The testing lab has reported that a faulty hydraulic meter on our Side-Thrust tester resulted in the premature rejection of the #1221 roller bearing. Design specifications call for 75 lbs of side thrust with a safety factor of X2. Retesting has already begun.

Courtesy: Larry Mielcarz, Consultant.

4.3.4 Test Reports

This type of report is an informal and inside report on a specific, one-of-a-kind test or testing problem. This is often a detailed account of the test results for a particular part of item. Or it could be a report about a problem with testing itself or setting up a test procedure. Many test reports originate at the engineering level of receiving materials such as steel or plastics. These materials must be tested and must conform to documented engineering drawings or specifications.

The structure of this type of report is as follows:

- Memo-report headings
- Purpose or problem
- Conditions
- Procedures and methods
- Conclusions
- Recommendations

Test Report

Date: ____________________

To: ____________________, Field Engineer

From: ____________________, Lab Technician

Subject: *Variable Frequency Drive Comparison Test*

Purpose of Test:
This test compares the breakdown (saturation) frequency and current output of the top three brands of variable frequency electronic drives. The comparisons are under a controlled environment with identical line and load conditions.

Conditions:
All three drives use PWM (Pulse Width Modulation) technology with microprocesser front ends for programming and setting parameters. All were programmed for 400Hz maximum frequency with a 60Hz knee/voltage setting. All drives use a common line power of 460V, 3-phase, and 60Hz, with 30A current-limiting fuses. All drives have identical motor loads rated at 15HP, 1800RPM, 460V, and 3-phase. All have NEMA 7 and 9 hazardous-location motor rating for Class I, Div. I, and Group C and D.

Procedure:
Current was measured with a clamp-on AC amp meter on the 0-30A scale setting, with readings on the incoming B phase of each drive. A grounding conductor was connected to the motor frame on each chassis and building ground conductor. Each electronic drive was started at 0Hz and increased in 1Hz increments until the amp meter read FLA (Full Load Amperage). In this test, the FLA was 21A. Individual current readings were also made at each motor's designed maximum frequency (172Hz).

Conclusions:
Brand C provided the best performance, with a maximum frequency of 206Hz and a minimum current draw of 18-7A at the designed maximum frequency of 175Hz.

Recommendations:
Standardize on brand C for all 175Hz design applications using the 1800RPM, 15HP motor.

Courtesy: Larry Mielcarz, Consultant.

4.3.5 Trip Reports

Travel is an expensive yet crucial element in modern industry. Technical experts often must travel long distances to monitor specialized equipment or to solve problems. A trip report provides a permanent record of the trip for future reference. It records the actions taken and accomplishments during the trip. The experience of one employee on the trip becomes available for other personnel in the future. The structure of a trip report is as follows:

- Memo-report headings
- Purpose of the trip
- Conclusions
- Actions taken
- Recommendations

Trip Report

Date: __________________

To: __________________, Quality Control Director

From: __________________, Product Manager

Subject: *Albuquerque VoTech Center (A.V.C.)*

Purpose of the Trip:
In September, Jim Vaughan, one of the A.V.C. instructors, told us that the five hydraulic student-training stations he had purchased in August of this year had developed leaks. He tried simply to tighten the fittings and gasket covers, but this did not stop the leaks. With no local tech-rep in the Albuquerque area, I made the side-trip to Albuquerque on my way to the Phoenix Training Products show.

Conclusions:
All five student-training stations have components that leaked at the point where the brass fittings thread into the sub-bases

and manifolds. On further examination, I found that these fittings were made without the use of some sort of pipe-thread compound. Four of the five training stations were leaking fluid at the Plexiglas covers on the front of the reservoirs.

Actions Taken:
I removed all the fittings on each training station and used 3/8-inch tape to seal the fittings in the sub-bases and manifolds. Pressure tests showed that all leaks were sealed with this action.

I drained each reservoir and removed the cover to find that in all cases, the 1-inch gaskets used to seal the reservoir wall and the Plexiglas cover had torn the bolt holes that run to the outside edge. I hand-cut new cover gaskets and hand-punched the bolt holes. After installing the gaskets and covers, I refilled the reservoirs and tested them under normal operating pressure. All leaks were stopped.

Recommendations:
1. Teflon tape may not be the optimum solution. We must use pipe-thread joint compound on future training-station manufacturing. We must also consider the thermal expansion between the brass fittings and the steel sub-bases.
2. We must purchase a hole punch of correct size for making the bolt holes in the Plexiglas cover gasket. As an alternative, we could possibly use a drill press and jig to pre-drill these holes with accuracy and care.

Courtesy: Larry Mielcarz, Consultant.

4.3.6 Trouble Reports

Sometimes a trouble report and a trip report are combined. In other cases, the trouble report describes a problem that did not entail travel. Trouble requiring a report comes in many forms, such as the following:

- Accidents
- Equipment failures

- Assembly line breakdowns
- Electronic communication problems
- Fire, flood, or storm damage

The structure of this type of report is as follows:

- Memo-report headings
- Problem description
- Action taken
- Recommendations

Trouble Report

Date: ____________________

To: ____________________, President

From: ____________________, Field Operations Manager

Subject: *Outside Sign Accident, 3/5/XX*

Problem:
On March 5, 19XX, two employees were assigned to clean and paint the Oak Tree Restaurant sign located on South Avenue. The men have a combined total of 22 years of experience. The sign is located on the northwest corner of the parking lot, about 28 feet above grade. As the men removed the sign's north face, a gust of wind blew it to the ground. Neither man was injured in the mishap. However, the sign's face was destroyed on impact. The sign has been replaced at a cost of $2,780.00, including labor.

In investigating the accident scene, I discovered that the crane-truck's sign-face saddle was still anchored to the truckbed. Both men admitted that they did not take the time to use the crane to lower the face to the ground. Instead, they decided to hand-carry the face down two parallel ladders set adjacent to the sign. The sign face measures 10 feet by 20 feet and weighs 207 lbs. As the wind came up, the combined strength of the two men was not enough to hold on to the face.

Action Taken:
According to written company policy, both men were suspended one day without pay and given a written reprimand.

Recommendations:
In order to counter what may be a growing complacency on the part of our installation crews, I would recommend the following:

- Require all crews to attend a general safety meeting every six months to review safety policies and procedures.
- Require all employees to watch our 20-minute video on safety procedures and OSHA requirements as they apply directly to our operation.

Courtesy: Larry Mielcarz, Consultant.

4.4 The Formal Report

Formal reports are the comprehensive documentation of major technical projects. By the nature of their scope and importance, they tend to be long and detailed. The actual scope and complexity of any particular formal report will depend on the substance of the report itself. Most formal reports are outside reports from one company to another. They cover many of the same subjects as inside memo-reports. The format varies greatly, depending on the company's standards and the nature of the report.

Because formal reports are more complex than memo-reports, they require a more formally structured format. The basic elements of a formal technical report are as follows:

1. Title page
2. Table of contents
3. Executive summary
4. Body (including all headings)
5. Conclusions
6. Recommendations
7. References
8. Bibliography
9. Appendixes
10. Glossary
11. Index

Not all formal reports will require every element. In some cases, various parts of these formal elements will become separate parts of the report and will stand alone. (See Exhibit 4–1 at the end of this section for an example of the structure of a formal report.)

4.4.1 Title Page

The title page can be arranged in a number of ways, but the basic elements must be there. These basic title elements are as follows:

- The full title of the report
- The name of the writer
- The writer's company
- The person or company receiving the report
- The date of the report

4.4.2 Table of Contents

The table of contents allows your reader to find the major elements of your report easily. The table itself is located at the front of the report just after the title page. *It is a direct reflection of your outline and is derived directly from it.* The table of contents contains all primary and secondary headings and topics as they appeared in your outline. As a general rule, you can go two levels deep into your outline for the table of contents.

Tables and figures are also contained in the table of contents but are listed separately. They are still part of the contents of the report, but to make the table of contents clearer, list tables and figures after the topic headings.

4.4.3 Executive Summary

In recent years, the executive summary has become the most common vehicle in reports to give a condensed overview of the report for the executive and managerial audience. It should be limited to a maximum of one or two pages. The biggest problem for managers today is staying informed. In most cases, managers simply do not have all the necessary technical understanding or enough time to stay informed. The primary purpose of the executive summary is to condense the report for those who do not have either the technical knowledge or the time to read the entire report.

The executive summary is *a managerial and not a technical* part of the report. The information is limited to the background, findings, and conclusions, along with the recommendations of the report. This summary should always be placed directly after the table of contents. In this way it is the first element of the report that the executive reader finds. Your executive summary should clearly summarize and condense the following information:

1. Background of opportunity or problem
2. Profit and/or cost implications

3. Findings and/or conclusions
4. Recommendations

4.4.4 Main Body or Discussion

The main body is the complete account of what you are writing about. The main body is often called a *discussion* because, as in an oral discussion, you will convert your structured ideas in outline form to flowing, conversational prose.

The main body of your report covers all the technical details of your subject as well as all the administrative results. This part of a report may contain any one or all three elements of technical writing: definition, description, and instruction. The organization of your report must reflect absolutely and in detail the outline you previously established.

4.4.5 Conclusions

The conclusions section puts the results and findings of your discussion in one place for your reader. The emphasis here is on what you have found in light of the purpose of the report and its implications. The implications here may be primarily technical or administrative or both. This will depend on the nature of the report.

4.4.6 Recommendations

The recommendations section is your opinion based on technical evidence and your expertise as a professional. It is what you the writer feel is the best course of action based on the report's conclusions and findings. The recommendations may be a technical course of action or they may be an administrative course of action or both.

4.4.7 References

You must document references if you quote from them directly or otherwise use their information. These references may be either placed at the bottom of the page where the reference appears, or placed together in a separate block section appearing at the end of the chapter, section, paper, etc.

4.4.8 Bibliography

This is an alphabetical list of all secondary sources you have used in preparing the report.

4.4.9 Appendixes

Appendixes are sections that contain supplemental information and documentation. This information is pertinent but not crucial to the report. It may also be information that is too detailed or voluminous to include in the main body of the text without impeding the orderly presentation of the main text. Typical information found in an appendix is as follows:

- charts
- graphs
- tables
- questionnaires

- correspondence
- interviews

4.4.10 Glossary

Your glossary contains selected technical terms and their definitions. These are terms that may possibly be unfamiliar to your readers. Your selection of terms will depend largely on your evaluation of your audience and its technical level of understanding.

The glossary should be set up in alphabetical order and in dictionary style.

4.4.11 Index

The index is an alphabetical, cross-referenced list of all topics and subjects of import contained in the report. Unlike the table of contents, an index will direct your reader to several related areas within a topic area.

Exhibit 4–1
Formal Report

[Title page]

High-Frequency 400Hz AC as an Alternative to Standard Low-Frequency 60Hz AC for Fluorescent Lighting Loads

By
L. A. Mielcarz
Technical Design Consultant

Prepared for
XYZ Development Corporation
Chicago, Illinois
July 1, 19XX

Table of Contents

Executive Summary

The purpose of this report is to determine the feasibility of a self-generated, high-frequency AC power source for fluorescent lighting.

Recent technology in high-frequency generation for fluorescent lighting loads has proven successful in various European countries. Such installations can reduce air-conditioning (cooling) loads, initial cost of lighting fixtures, fixture maintenance, and general energy consumption. This report examines the application of this technology in the new bank and office complex in North Phoenix.

Lighting Load A total of 7,472 fixtures with energy-saving lamps will cause a total load of 2,830,900 kwhr. This will cost $184,008.00.

Ballast Heat The heat generated by the 13,852 ballasts in the building will total 620,157 Btu. Annual cost to remove this heat with the air-conditioning system is projected at $29,575.00.

Fixture Cost Comparison Standard fixture costs total $314,766.00. High-frequency costs total $297, 212.00. The difference between the two is $17,554.00.

Fixture Maintenance Comparison Estimated standard fixture maintenance will cost $29,888.00 annually. Estimated high-frequency fixture maintenance will cost $16,812.00 annually. The difference between the two is $13,076.00.

Generator Costs A 1,500kw three-phase generator (alternator) has an initial cost of $646,580.00. Its projected annual energy consumption is $158,600.00. The estimated annual maintenance cost on this generator is $12,500.00

Installation Costs Installation cost for the generator and main switchgear only is estimated at $132,500.00. Dedicated wireways and lighting panels for the high-frequency distribution system are estimated at $283,750.00

Cost Analysis of Both Systems A high-frequency self-generated system will cost more than a standard system. The difference in system costs is $1,045,276.00. The annual energy and labor savings will be $55,559.00 based on present energy and labor costs.

Conclusions Payback is projected to be 18.8 years. The payback is figured in terms of energy savings, reduced lighting maintenance, and reduced fixture costs.

Recommendations Based on a projected property holding time of eight years, the payback period is far too great and would incur investment loss. Use traditional wiring methods and public power for all energy uses in the building.

2

Detailed Discussion

Purpose of Study

The purpose of this report is to determine whether a self-generated, high-frequency AC power source (generator/alternator) can be used at the XYZ Development complex in North Phoenix. This report will determine whether the self-generated system can be economically installed, operated, and maintained. It will determine whether the system can provide sufficient energy savings to pay for itself over a feasible period, based on a projected eight-year property ownership.

Background

In correspondence dated January X, 19XX, Jane Reynolds, Manager and CEO of XYZ Development Corporation, mentioned her observations during a recent trip to Europe of lighting generation at several major hotels. The hotels were using self-generated, high-frequency (400Hz) AC power supplies.

These supplies powered the fluorescent lighting loads in the hotels and in adjacent buildings. The main purpose for such electrical distribution is the ability to ignite fluorescent lamps without the use of traditional iron-core and coil ballasts. By eliminating the ballasts, the system also eliminates the heat given off by the ballasts. This results in reducing the overall cooling system load, initial fixture cost, ballast maintenance, and replacement cost of ballasts.

The question remains whether it is feasible to use this dedicated system of power generation for fluorescent lighting in the proposed 18-story, 720,000 sq. ft. bank and office complex in North Phoenix. If such a system is installed, it must be done in the early stages of construction. Consequently, this study will try to facilitate a decision at this early stage of development.

Lighting Load

All fixtures will use 34-watt, energy-saving lamps. Each fixture will average 2,500 hours of operation. Over the length of a year, the total kilowatt-hours consumed will be 2,830,900 (7,472 fixtures using energy-saving lamps). Based on a charge of 6.5 cents per kwhr, total annual energy costs for the fluorescent lighting will be $184,008.00. See Appendix A.

Ballast Heat

The total number of ballasts for the fluorescent lighting fixtures is 13,852. Using industry standards, each ballast gives off 44.77btu of heat. The total heat output for all ballasts comes to 620,154btu. Because 1kw equals 3,412btu, the ballast heat represents 182kw of cooling load over the span of 2,500 hours. This represents a total energy cost of $29,575.00 in order to remove the ballast heat.

[Remaining sections of Discussion are omitted.]

Conclusions

Payback is projected to be 18.8 years. This payback period is figured in terms of energy savings, reduced lighting maintenance, and reduced fixture costs.

Recommendations

Based on a projected property-holding time of eight years, the payback period is far too great and would incur investment loss. Use traditional wiring methods and public power for all energy uses in the complex.

Appendix A

Lighting Fixture Energy Cost Table[1]

Fixture Style	Quantity	Load in VA's per unit	Load in Kilowatts per unit
F-40EW 2-LAMP	1,102	82 VA	83kw
F-40EW 4-LAMP	6,380	164 VA	1,046kw
F-40EW 1-LAMP	80	42 VA	3.36kw
Total Fluorescent Load			1,132.36kw

[1] National Fire Protection Association, eds. *National Electrical Code 1993.* (Quincy, MA: Delmar Publishers Inc., 1993) 70–71.

[Because there is only one footnoted source, it would most likely be put at the bottom of the page on which it appears.]

Bibliography

National Fire Protection Association, eds. *National Electrical Code 1993*. Quincy, MA: Delmar Publishers, 1993.

Spradlin, William H., Jr. *The Building Estimators Reference Book*. Chicago: Frank R. Walker Co., 1986.

Summers, Wilford I. *American Electricians Handbook, 12th Ed*. New York: McGraw-Hill, Inc., 1992.

Glossary

AC (alternating current). Alternating current is electricity measured in terms of current that constantly changes polarity. For example, sixty-cycle current is current that changes polarity 60 times per second.

Alternator. An alternator is a device or machine that causes current to alternate and usually requires a prime mover like an internal combustion engine to provide the power to turn the alternator.

Dedicated Wireway. A dedicated wireway is a channel for electrical wiring in a building as listed in the National Electrical Code. Metal or plastic conduit is a common example of dedicated wireway in commercial buildings.

Switchgear. A switchgear is an enclosure designed specifically for the distribution of electrical power through the use of switches, fuses, current breakers, and bus bars.

Section 5

FORMS OF TECHNICAL WRITING II: Proposals, Manuals, and Journal Articles

5.1 The Technical Proposal

A proposal is a selling document that advocates the purchase of a company's products or services. It can also come from within a single company and advocate the purchase of equipment or hiring of additional personnel. Proposals from one company to another generally tend to be lengthy and complex. Proposals that are generated within a single company tend to be brief and simple. In either case, your audience will be primarily managerial. As a result, you will need to take special care to describe and define terms and concepts.

If a proposal is solicited, it will be a mirror of an RFP (request for proposal). If the proposal is unsolicited, it will reflect the thinking of the firm seeking the contract and its estimate of what the receiving company requires.

It is very important to keep in mind that a proposal is a selling document. It must persuade the receiving company to buy the goods or services. Unlike a feasibility report, a proposal is biased in favor of the project.

The following is a typical format for a proposal:

- Cover letter
- Table of contents
- Executive summary
- Proposed program
- Company background
- Budget
- Appendixes (optional as needed)

Exhibit 5–1 is a proposal for a computer software program. Notice that the document explains the program's capabilities and sells the reader on the program and vendor.

5.2 The Technical Manual

The primary reason for writing a technical manual is to document a process or mechanism or a combination of the two. Through documentation in the manual, the elements of a process or mechanism are defined and described, and instructions for its use are provided. This use can cover such things as operation, maintenance, servicing, and repair.

There are many types of technical manuals. The most prevalent types of manuals are operations manuals, user manuals, and maintenance manuals.

Exhibit 5–1
Technical Proposal

MIDWEST
INFORMATION SOLUTIONS

Business solutions for success in the 90's **[Cover letter]**

October 26, 1992

Mr. Gary Norman
ABC Products, Inc.
P.O. Box 1414
2600 Forest Avenue
Milwaukee, WI 53207

Dear Mr. Norman:

Midwest Information Solutions in conjunction with Northwest Information Systems takes great pleasure in providing this proposal to meet your distribution management needs. The proposal is structured to provide a business solution that is price and performance competitive and that will enable the efficient implementation of the best software and hardware solutions.

Our understanding of your objectives and requirements is based on the Request For Proposal (RFP) received at our offices on October 13, 1992.

We would like to express our appreciation for the opportunity to present this information for your consideration.

While MIS will act as the prime contractor for the system being proposed, Northwest Information Systems, Inc. will assist in the installation of the software and in the design of any software modifications that may be required to meet your business needs.

Sincerely,

Lawrence P. Ott, President
Encl.

Proposal For ABC Products, Inc.

Presented by:

Midwest Information Solutions, Inc.

Table of Contents

[Omitted from exhibit for length.] (2.2–2.42)

[Omitted from exhibit for length.] (4)

Executive Summary

[Executive summary]

Application Software

The Inventory Management Accounting Control System (IMACS) has been developed to provide the most advanced user-friendly distribution and financial business system on the market today. Integrated with the PICK operating system, UNIX and associated software, including the Database Retrieval Language, the application software is supported by a highly trained and motivated professional staff. Their experience in distribution and financial accounting ensures that implementation can be carried out efficiently and effectively.

The combination, within the software product, of Sales Order, Inventory Management, Pricing, Purchase Order Control, Sales Analysis, and Financial Management systems provides the ideal method for the effective planning and control of all resources within a distribution organization. The systems are totally integrated, enabling data entered into one software module to be immediately available for use in any other module. This flexibility provides you with maximum control over your own installation in terms of investment, implementation, and other specific needs.

Hardware

We are proposing an NCR/ADDS System 3000 Model 3447 to fulfill the demand for a state-of-the-art hardware platform that allows for the integration of a central processor with PCs, faxes, terminals and several types of printers. It provides the processing power to meet your present needs and also provides for projected future expansion. The NCR/ADDS platform combines the features of the PICK database with the communication and networking features of UNIX into an integrated environment. The result is a proven system with the latest technology.

The IMACS Distribution System combined with the well-proven hardware platforms from NCR/ADDS provides a composite offering, the benefits of which cannot be obtained elsewhere.

Technical Proposal

[Proposed program]

Software Requirements Checklist

Standard software will satisfy requirements.
Software modification necessary to satisfy requirement.
Will not be provided.

2.000 Order Entry and Invoicing

2.100 Order Entry

Standard	Modification	Not provided	No.	Requirement
⊗	○	○	2.101	Multiple "canned" comments available at several order-entry points.
⊗	○	○	2.102	Back-order preference entered on order.
○	⊗	○*	2.103	Yard orders entered will "suggest" tally based on formula, and allowing for adapting to current inventory or salesman's specifications.
○	⊗	○	2.104	Orders to mills can have various relative values placed on each length which computer will spread based on quantities of each length for internal costing purposes.
○	⊗	○	2.105	Option to indicate on order when entered that other certain traders should receive E Mail notice of the item # sold and time of day.
⊗	○	○	2.106	Computer calculates est. profit on each order. Est. profit reflects costs such as special dating, handling charges, etc.
○	⊗	○	2.107	Orders can coordinate and cross-reference multiple vendors and customers on one truck or rail car. Display ETA of inbound stock including tracing report.
○	⊗	○	2.108	Several "order books" on screen to assign sequential order numbers.
⊗	○	○	2.109	Handle: Regular charge orders, cash sales, credit and returns, direct ships, blanket orders, hold and bill, will call, delivered orders, work orders, deferred orders, C.O.D. orders, credit checking (including open orders).
⊗	○	○	2.110	Automatically commit stock at order entry.
⊗	○	○	2.111	Easily create purchase orders for unsold direct purchases.
⊗	○	○	2.112	Tie yard orders to takers, report productivity by division.
⊗	○	○	2.113	Good special order-type handling.
⊗	○	○	2.114	Yard ticket printing can be extra large.

* A "tally" system is on the IMACS "Product Development" calendar.

2.11 Additional software features included in IMACS that were not listed in the Software Checklist.

- "Hot Keys" provide the ability to "jump" to another function, perform a required task, and return to the starting point and complete that task.
- "Auto" PO's. This feature provides the ability to use sales history, open order status, PO history, vendor minimums, and other key data to develop recommended PO's. The PO can then be modified if desired prior to printing.
- An extensive "Pricing" system that provides multiple options with least price, first price, or rolling price selection in Order Entry.
- A "Profit Control" option that requires all "override" prices in Order Entry to conform to a set "Profit" percentage.
- Extensive Sales Analysis with the ability to create custom relationships between the Inventory, Customer, Vendor, and other criteria for reporting purposes.

2.12 Other "Systems" experience

- IMACS can be implemented in several differing environments including the PICK/UNIX environment. Another option is a UNIX-based relational database called Universe. We feel that the PICK/-UNIX option offers a more "User Friendly" environment, while providing the added functionality of UNIX.
- IMACS has been integrated with UNIX and PC applications through GUI type interfaces for the purpose of exhanging data. The NCR/-ADDS hardware is considered to be an "Open System" and supports "Client Server" technology such as X-Windows.

[Sections are omitted here for length.]

[Company background]

2.5 Vendor Background and Qualifications

Midwest Information Solutions, Inc.
Although only in business as Midwest Information Solutions for four months, the staff of MISI includes over 17 years of experience in the PICK Operating System, as both dealer and end-user. The MISI staff includes:

Larry Ott, President, who has held the position of
President at R-Computer Company, Inc. and
director of MIS for Serta Incorporated

Susan Novak, formerly of R-Computer and Improved
Insurance Systems, Inc. Susan is experienced in
Finance and Administration as well as Customer
Service and Technical Support

In addition to IMACS, Midwest Information Solutions offers custom programming and modifications as well as a wide range of new and used hardware and peripherals.

Northwest Information Systems, Inc.

Now in their 13th year of operation, NISI has gained the reputation of delivering the right combination of industry knowledge and state-of-the-art technology required to produce successful business solutions. At this time, there are 175 installations of IMACS on the East and West Coasts.

Seattle, New Jersey, Cincinnati, Atlanta, and Illinois locations provide sales and support services offering your firm complete service and support with assured follow-up. Marketing, Product Development, and Management functions are located in NISI's Seattle area office, where more than half of the 25 employees are devoted to Applications and Customer Support.

3 Cost Proposal **[Budget]**

Cost Worksheet Software	*Non-Recurring* Standard Software	Modification/ Development	Annual Recurring Maintenance Cost
Application Software			
1.0 Sales Support	$ incl.	$ none	$ incl.
2.0 Order Entry and Invoicing	$ incl.	$ *	$ incl.
3.0 Inventory and Warehouse Control	$ incl.	$ none	$ incl.
4.0 Traffic	$ N/A	$ *	$ **
5.0 Accounts Receivable	$ incl.	$ none	$ incl.
6.0 Commissions	$ incl.	$ *	$ **
7.0 Purchasing	$ incl.	$ none	$ incl.

8.0	Accounts Payable	$ incl.	$ none	$ incl.
9.0	General Ledger	$ incl.	$ none	$ incl.
10.0	Remanufacturing/Milling	$ N/A	$ *	$ **
11.0	Reload	incl.	none	incl.
32 User IMACS Total Package		$51,840.00***	*	$ 8,300 yr. 2

* Cost of modifications would be quoted after a detailed specification has been developed.

** Modifications are supported as an addendum to the standard support agreement at a rate of 15% per year of the cost of the modification.

*** Includes first-year support and maintenance fees.

Source: Midwest Information Solutions, Inc.

5.2.1 Technical Operations and User Manuals

Operations manuals are meant primarily for the user or purchaser of equipment. This type of manual tells the user how to use the equipment in the intended fashion. The manual will make extensive use of technical description and technical instruction. You must write it simply and clearly, because the technical level of the user is generally lower than the level of expertise of those who designed and/or manufactured the equipment.

The examples that follow show an operations manual (Exhibit 5–2) and a user manual (Exhibit 5–3). The operations manual is for a piece of electronic testing equipment called a *digital multimeter* and is written for the student or apprentice in the field of electronics. The user manual is for a software program on a mainframe computer. This user manual is written for the new users of the software and non-specialists. Notice that neither manual condescends to its reader, yet both consider readers' lack of technical expertise.

5.2.2 Technical Maintenance Manuals

Maintenance manuals are meant primarily for the highly technical expert who repairs and maintains a piece of equipment. These manuals heavily rely on such tools as schematics and performance graphs. Visuals such as these take advanced understanding and expertise in the specific technical field.

Exhibit 5–4 shows a manual for the maintenance of a piece of electronic testing equipment called a MOSFET Multimeter. To use this meter effectively and to maintain it require specialized technical knowledge and training.

The structural format of most technical manuals is as follows:

- Title cover page
- Preface/introduction
- Table of contents
- Mechanism descriptions
- Process descriptions
- User instructions
- Appendixes
- Glossaries
- Indexes

Exhibit 5–2
Technical Operations Manual

[Title cover page]

OPERATION INFORMATION FOR THE

DIGITAL MULTIMETER NO. 50200A/50220A

Introduction

[Preface/introduction]

This manual provides operating instructions and practical information for the Energy Concepts Digital Multimeter, Model No. 50200A/50220A. Read this manual thoroughly before you operate the unit. Information on the Digital Multimeter is also included in the *Maintenance Information for the Digital Multimeter*, book number 50208A.

Every effort has been made to design dependability, accuracy, and durability into each unit. New products are being designed constantly to meet the needs of both education and the service industries. We welcome your comments about our test equipment and other products.

It is both a privilege and a pleasure serving you.

Richard E. Gibbons
President, Energy Concepts, Inc.

[Table of contents]

Table of Contents

[Omitted from exhibit for length.]

[Omitted from exhibit for length.]

[Mechanism descriptions]

Section 1: Operating Information

General

The Energy Concepts Digital Multimeter is an easily operated, versatile instrument for students and technicians in all laboratory applications. The unit is self-contained, line operated, and features advanced solid-state design.

The electrical quantities being measured are read from the 3 1/2-digit Digital Display on the front panel. You can measure six separate functions, with each function having several different ranges. You will use the CURRENT section of the multimeter to make current measurements. Use the VOLTS/OHMS section for voltage and resistance measurements. You may select the function by pressing one of the six blue pushbuttons between the range switches. Press only one of these switches at any given time.

Additional features of the Digital Multimeter include full input protection against overloads. The Digital Display is isolated from the input circuitry, and is fully protected from sudden overloads. The current input is circuit-breaker protected against overload. The power indicator LED flashes in case the breaker has been tripped. The Volts/Ohms input is protected internally to 1000 V on Volts functions, and to 300 Volts on Ohms functions.

Front Panel Controls

The following paragraphs contain a description of each control and receptacle. The descriptions are keyed to the encircled numbers in Figure 1-1, which is a front view of the Digital Multimeter.

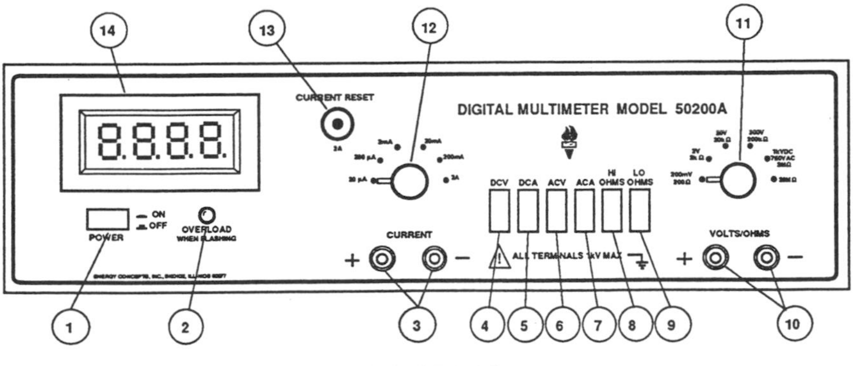

FIGURE 1–1: Front Panel of Digital Multimeter

1. Power Switch
Use this red pushbutton switch to apply power from the AC line to the unit. Press the switch to the in position to turn it ON. Then press it to the out position to turn it OFF.

2. Current Overload Indicator
The "overload when flashing" LED has two purposes. It indicates that the digital multimeter has power when the LED glows steadily. It flashes on and off after an overload involving a current function occurs. Pressing the CURRENT RESET button (item 13) should cause the LED to glow steadily, providing that the condition that caused the overload has been corrected.

3. Current Terminals
Plug the positive input lead into the red terminal (+) and plug the negative input lead into the black terminal (-) when measuring DC current. Use either leads with either terminal when measuring AC current.

[Sections are omitted for length.]

14. Digital Display
This 3 1/2 digit Digital Display shows numbers from 000 to 1999. When you select a range, the decimal point shifts as required. When you apply a negative voltage, a negative sign precedes the number. On the other hand, the number is positive when no sign precedes the number. No polarity sign will show for AC or resistance readings.

Preparation for Use

The Energy Concepts Digital Multimeter is portable. It can be placed on any flat, vibration-free surface for satisfactory operation. The Digital Multimeter operates in a closed case, so venting is not necessary. However, space at the front of the instrument should permit electrical connections to the input terminals and changing modes of operation.

The operator should understand thoroughly the functions of all the controls, terminals, and indicators before proceeding with the meter setup and operation.

Place the instrument in the desired operating location. Then connect the AC power cable to an appropriate 50/60 Hz source. The input power is normally for 120 VAC unless 230 VAC is specifically requested.

[Sections are omitted for length.]

[User instructions]

Operating Procedure

General

1. When measuring current (AC or DC), always connect the multimeter in SERIES with the circuit. Low frequency (less than 1 kHz) AC current measurements do not require observing polarity when connecting the test leads to a circuit. However, you must observe polarity with DC current measurements. All currents are measured through separate input terminals.
2. When measuring voltage (AC or DC), always connect the multimeter in PARALLEL with the circuit. AC voltage measurements do not require observing polarity when connecting the test leads to a circuit. However, polarity must be observed with DC voltage measurements.
3. Whenever a voltage, resistance, or current is unknown, begin with the Range Switch set to the highest range position. Then, after observing the first reading, you may rotate the Range Switch to a lower range position (if warranted) for a more accurate reading.
4. You can switch between voltage and current functions without removing the test leads from the circuit. Use the correct input terminals for voltage and current. However, remove the test leads from an active circuit when using the OHMS function.
5. When performing current measurements, the test leads should be connected to, or disconnected from, the circuit measuring points only while the circuit under test is de-energized.

The following steps comprise a general outline and are common to Digital Multimeter use for any measurement function. The instructions just given must also be considered in the operation.

1. Plug the power cord into the AC line. Then push in the red POWER switch (item 1) to apply AC power to the unit.
2. Select the mode of meter operation by pressing in the appropriate blue pushbutton (items 4 through 9). Disregard the random numbers appearing on the Digital Display.
3. Select the range of measurements by proper setting of the appropriate RANGE switch (item 11 or 12).
4. Insert the test leads into the proper set of red and black terminals (item 3 or 10), observing polarity if measuring DC voltage or current.

5. Connect the test leads to the proper points in the circuit being measured.

6. Read the actual measurement from the Digital Display.

Important aspects of these various measurements will be considered in the next sections of this manual. These sections give specific instructions for using the Digital Multimeter as a voltmeter, an ohmmeter, and an ammeter.

[Sections are omitted for length.]

Source: Energy concepts, Inc.

Exhibit 5–3
Technical User Manual

[Title cover page]

Warehousing User Guide
Volume III

[Table of contents]

Contents

[Omitted from exhibit for length.]

[Omitted from exhibit for length.]

1. Overview

1.1 Audience and Structure **[Preface/introduction]**

This guide is the third of three volumes intended for warehouse personnel. The procedures described in this manual assume the installation of Outbound Control, Order Maintenance (Front End Repository), Store Order Processing, and Order Based Replenishment.

Volume Three focuses on the final phase of the warehousing process and includes the following sections:

- Overview
- Outbound Control/Order Maintenance
- Store Order Processing/Billing
- Replenishment
- Reports

1.2 Conventions

The following conventions are used throughout this Guide:

- When you are instructed to press a key, the key name will appear in capital letters and bold type. For example, when instructed to press the Enter key, the text will read, "Press **ENTER**."
- The Tab key enables movement from field to field. If a field is completely filled, the cursor will automatically move you to the next enterable position.
- All field definitions are broken into two categories:

  >> *Non-Enterable fields*—These are fields that are display only; you cannot enter or change the data. The majority of non-enterable fields directly follow the header information. (Header information is described in section 4 of the manual *Introduction to DCS2000 Logistics Systems*.

  << *Enterable fields*—These are fields in which you can enter or change data.

1.4 Concepts **[Process descriptions]**

[Sections are omitted for length.]

1.4.1 System Prerequisites and Data Requirements Outbound Control and Order Based Replenishment are prerequisites for the Store Order

Processing system. Therefore, you may not add Store Order Processing unless Outbound Control and Order Based Replenishment are installed per BACG system specifications and defined to DCS2000 via Warehouse Maintenance/Package Options Control (Conversion 402). When installed, Order Maintenance (Front End Repository) must be run with Outbound Control.

DCS2000 Development Support is required for all the BACG systems.

As in most systems, the validity and interrelationships of the data determine how well the systems will perform for you. (A summary of the data elements and where they are maintained can be found at the end of this section.)

The data can be specified and found in one of the three types of files:

- Online Maintained Files—designated by conversation number—Data can be changed anytime using existing DCS2000 conversations.
- Compile-Time Tables—designated by table number (DCST##)—Data is initialized in tables that are not changed frequently. If there are changes required, the programs accessing the tables need to be recompiled after the changes are made.
- Other System Maintained Files—designated by parameter records—Data is created and maintained using these files.

Several of the critical/prerequisite files are fully documented outside of this User Guide and are referenced where applicable:

- Conversation 402—Warehousing and OCT Maintenance, which contains the Warehousing and Purchasing Option Control Tables (OCTs), is described in the *DCS2000 System Parameter User Guide*. An example of the Store Order Processing OCT screen follows:

```
D0603M1    600 ADD             ITEM MAINTENANCE                 04/24/92 16.53
LAST CHNG 00000             STORE ORDER INFORMATION
                  LOC: 901  GROCRY        STATUS: NI

ITEM#: 00920                             BUYER: 17900   CHRIS YEAGER
DESC: DIET CHOC MOUSSE ENV                      SIZE: 6 OZ       PACK: 1
UPC:  0000000000000000000          VENDOR: 0900      N-INN: 1     RPCK: 1

LOAD TYPE...........: GM                 RETAIL CASE PRICE..: .00
TAX FLAG............: N                  ------------- RETAILS -------------
HAZARDOUS FLAG......: NO                  @@@@ FOR    AMOUNT      COST MARKUP
                                           1   0      .000           .000
                                           2   0      .000           .000
ORDER UNIT..........: S                    3   0      .000           .000
ORDER MINIMUM.......: 1                    4   0      .000           .000
ORDER MAXIMUM.......: 99999                5   0      .000           .000
PALLET FLAG.........: N                                  DLY         WTD
ROUNDING %..........: 0                  SHIPMENTS.......: 0          0
                                         OUT-OF-STOCKS..: 0           0
SUB TO ITEM#........:                    ADJUSTMENTS....: 0           0
SUB TYPE / PERCENT..:    / .00           SCRATCHES......: 0           0

                            PF11=UPDATE
```

```
D0604M1   600  ADD            ITEM MAINTENANCE            04/24/92  17.20
LAST CHNG 00000             DISTRIBUTION / SECURITY
                  LOC: 901  GROCRY        STATUS: NEW

ITEM#: 00920                             BUYER: 17900   MARC RICCIO
DESC: DIET CHOC MOUSSE ENV                      SIZE: 6 OZ       PACK: 1
UPC:  0000000000000000000          VENDOR: 0900      N-INN: 1     RPCK: 1
               DISTRIBUTION     AA..  A...  B...  C...  D...  E...
                  DATES
  WAREHOUSE :
  REGULAR ..:                   10    8     6     4     4     2
  PUSH .....:



 SETUP ......:
 DISCONTINUE :

              ----------------SECURITY CLEARANCE----------------
              A B C D E F G H I J K L M N O P Q R S T U V W X Y Z
                X                       X                       X

                         PF11=UPDATE
```

[User instructions]

1.4.2 Store Polling The creation of store orders at the store level is the client's responsibility. Normally, these orders are transmitted to a central processing facility and edited. At this point, the orders can be loaded into the Repository and other client-specific edit checks (i.e., for data entry errors, etc.) can be performed.

The client has the option of having all or selected orders go to the Repository. After the initial edits, the client can decide, based upon load and/or order dates, to allow orders without any errors to bypass the Repository and be loaded directly into the Raw Orders file. As a result, only orders with data entry errors will go to the Repository. If the OCT, LOAD ALL ORDERS TO REPOSITORY (Conversation 402), is set to Y (yes), then all orders will be loaded to the Repository; if set to N (no), then all orders with a scheduled load and/or order date today will be loaded to the Raw Orders file and the rest will go to the Repository.

Source: BACG, Inc.

Exhibit 5–4
Technical Maintenance Manual

MAINTENANCE INFORMATION FOR THE

MOSFET MULTIMETER
No. 50500/50520

INTRODUCTION

This manual provides maintenance information for the Energy Concepts MOSFET Multimeter, Model No. 50500/50520. This manual also includes circuit board information, various required adjustments, parts lists, a schematic diagram, and other information used for proper maintenance and troubleshooting of the unit. Operational information for the MOSFET Multimeter is also in the manual titled, *Operation Information for the MOSFET Multimeter,* manual No. 50509.

Each new multimeter has been inspected, adjusted, and tested before shipment from the factory. Upon receipt of your MOSFET Multimeter inspect the shipping carton and the equipment for damage. Report any visible damage to your local carrier for repair or replacement. If the multimeter does not function properly or if there is some question about how it should operate contact the Energy Concepts Service Center for additional information.

This instrument is backed by more than sixty years of experience in designing and manufacturing educational and practical training equipment. Every effort has been made to design into each unit a maximum degree of dependability, accuracy, and durability. New products are being designed constantly to meet the needs of both education and the service industries. We welcome comments that you may have about our products or test equipment.

It is both a privilege and a pleasure to continue serving you.

Richard E. Gibbons
President, Energy Concepts, Inc.

Table of Contents

[omitted from exhibit for length.]

Maintenance Information

General

The Energy Concepts MOSFET Multimeter is a precision instrument. When used and maintained properly, the ECI MOSFET Multimeter will provide years of trouble-free operation. The chassis parts and circuit board components are easily accessible and clearly identified for convenience in troubleshooting. NOTE: ALL TROUBLESHOOTING, COMPONENT REPLACEMENT, AND ALIGNMENT OF THIS INSTRUMENT SHOULD BE PERFORMED BY AUTHORIZED, QUALIFIED SERVICE PERSONNEL ONLY.

Case Removal

1. Disconnect the AC power cable from the AC source. Remove all leads from the front panel.
2. Use a 9/64" Allen wrench to remove the four Allen-head cap screws from the end caps.
3. Lay the caps to one side. Remove the front panel and panel-mounted components by sliding the unit forward out of the case.

Circuit Board Component Identification

Figure 1 shows the electrical components mounted on the top of the circuit board. Use Figure 1 to locate and identify the various mounted components. The foil on the bottom of the circuit board is also shown (superimposed) to aid in visualizing the electrical connections.

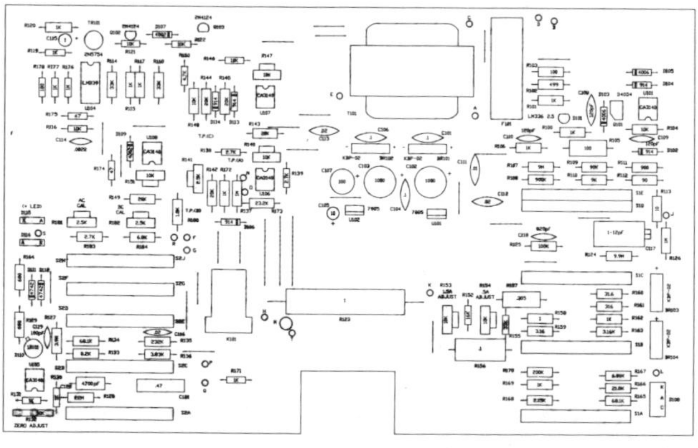

FIGURE 1: Circuit Board, Component Side

Figure 2 shows the electrical components viewed from the bottom of the circuit board. Now, the components on the top are superimposed to aid in visualizing the electrical connections.

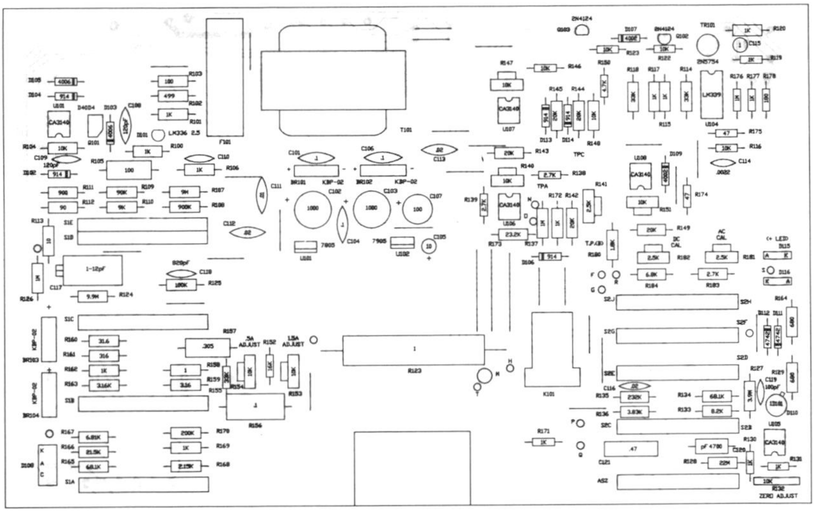

FIGURE 2: Circuit Board, Foil Side

Internal Fuses

The MOSFET Multimeter is equipped with an internal line protection fuse. The 1/4A fuse located on the circuit board protects the unit from transformer failure or severe line voltage variations.

Calibration Procedure

General

This MOSFET Multimeter has been factory calibrated to the specifications listed in this manual. However, the instrument may require recalibration after a period of routine use, or as a result of component change or replacement. Before attempting to calibrate this instrument, you must be sure the unit is operating properly. All malfunctions must be corrected. Refer to the MOSFET Operation Manual to determine the operating conditions of the instrument.

The MOSFET Multimeter is designed for high sensitivity on low ranges. This sensitivity combined with the high impedance input (10M ohm), results in an electrostatic pickup on the lower AC voltage ranges (0.05 to 1.5 V).

In normal operation the meter pointer may deflect upscale when the unshielded test leads are not in use. When the probe tips of the test leads are shorted together, or connected in a circuit for measuring, the meter pointer will return to zero.

On occasion, this high sensitivity will cause the instrument to go into an overload condition. This could be a result of one or more of the following:

1. Unshielded test leads lying parallel to an AC power cable.
2. Handling the unshielded test leads.
3. Physically touching the metal probe tips.
4. Close proximity to fluorescent lighting fixtures, industrial machinery, etc.

Preliminary

1. Remove the instrument from its case.
2. Connect the AC power cable to a 120 volt, 50/60 Hz AC source. Do not depress the AC On/Off switch at this time. Extreme caution should be used when handling this instrument once the AC power cable is plugged in.
3. Mechanically zero the meter pointer with the instrument in its normal upright operating position.
4. Depress the AC On/Off switch to apply AC power to the instrument.

Eelectrical Zero Adjust

NOTE

PERFORMING THE ELECTRICAL ZEROING PROCEDURE DOES NOT AFFECT CALIBRATION. THE PROCEDURE AFFECTS POTENTIOMETERS R140, R147, R151 AND THE FRONT PANEL ZERO ADJUST.

Figure 3 shows the location of the trimpots.

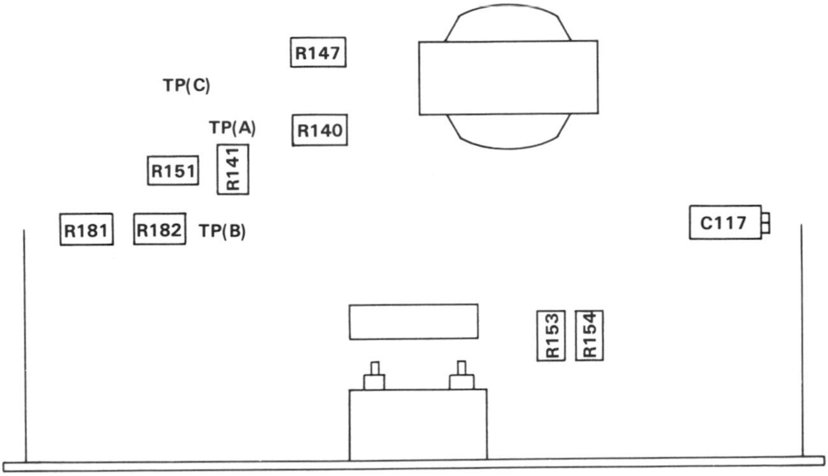

FIGURE 3: Location of Trimpots

1. Short test point A (T.P.A.) to the black input terminal. Do not short the input terminals at this time.
2. If this procedure is performed after a major repair, preset R140, R147, R151 and the front panel ZERO ADJUST potentiometers to mid range. This step is not required if you are fine tuning.
3. Place the function selector in one of the OHMs positions.
4. Adjust R140 for zero on the meter.
5. Keep test point A shorted. Short test points B and C to the black input terminal.
6. Place the FUNCTION selector in the DCV position.
7. Adjust R151 for zero on the meter.
8. Disconnect the short from test point C.
9. Adjust R147 for zero on the meter.
10. Disconnect the test leads from test points A and B.
11. Place a short jumper across the input terminals and place the RANGE selector in the 0.05 V position.
12. Rotate the ZERO ADJUST control on the front panel until the meter dips to zero.

13. While rotating the RANGE switch through each position, verify that the pointer stays within 1/2 division of zero. If it does not, repeat this procedure starting with step 1. Remove the jumper from the input terminals.

Troubleshooting

Integrated circuits are more sensitive to abuse than vacuum tubes, gas tubes, etc. But, ICs, when operated within their ratings and protected from abuse, are more trouble free. The failure of an IC can usually be traced to some cause other than the IC itself. Some causes of failure in semiconductors are excessive supply voltage, excessive input signals, reversed polarities, improper heat sinking, improper ventilation, and transients. However, with the MOSFET Multimeter, the most probable cause of semiconductor breakdown will be excessive supply voltage and deterioration due to the age of the device.

The internal fusing should be checked before troubleshooting any piece of equipment. This is particularly true for the MOSFET Multimeter. Because the wire within the fuse is not easily seen, an ohmmeter should be used to check for an open. This should be done with the fuse out of its holder.

If the meter does not indicate, verify that the positive and negative power supplies have the proper voltage and that the relay is pulling in. Table 2 shows the relationship between inputs and labeled test points.

TABLE 2: Inputs and Test Points

INPUT	TEST POINT A	TEST POINT B	TEST POINT C
(+) Full Scale .05, .5, 5, 50, and 500 V 50 µA, 50 mA, and 500 mA	50 mV	1.2 V	–1.2 V
(–) Full Scale .05, .5, 5, 50, and 500 V 50 µA, 50 mA, and 500 mA	–50 mV	–1.2 V	0
AC Full Scale .05, .5, 5, 50, and 500 V 50 µA, 50 mA, and 500 mA	42 mVAC	1.0 VAC	–.46 V
OHMS, Shorted Inputs	–50 mV approx.	–1.2 V approx.	n/a
LO OHMS, Shorted Input	–50 mV approx.	–1.2 V approx.	n/a

Should it become necessary to check the meter movement itself, first turn off the Multimeter. Disconnect all meter wires. Next, measure the DC resistance. It should be about 4.4 KΩ. If the meter conforms to these values, it is working properly.

Table 3 shows the common problems involved with the MOSFET Multimeter. It also includes the most likely cause of problems and how to correct them. Repair work should not begin without a thorough knowledge of the circuits.

TABLE 3: Common MOSFET Multimeter Problems

PROBLEM	PROBABLE CAUSES	REPAIR TO BE DONE
No meter indication on any range.	Fuse F101 - Relay - Q102 - Triac TR101 - Meter M1	Replace defective component.
With the input shorted, FUNCTION switch in DCV, ACV, DCA, or ACV, the meter does not remain at zero in all the positions of the RANGE switch.	Potentiometers R132, 140, 147, and 151 are misaligned Op-amps U105 - U106 - U107 - U108	Perform the electrical zeroing procedure. Replace defective component.
Ohmmeter function is inoperative.	Op-amp U103 - reference diode D101	Replace defective component.
Polarity indicators inoperative.	Comparator U104 - LEDs D115 - D116	Replace defective component.
Overload not being detected.	Comparator U104 - Triac TR101	Replace defective component.
Overload indicator inoperative.	LED D108	Replace defective component.
Amps function inoperative.	Limiting resistor R123 - Protection bridges BR103 - BR104	Replace defective component.

Service Parts List

P.C. Board Parts

SCHEMATIC REFERENCE NUMBER	PART NUMBER	COMPONENT DESCRIPTION
		Transistors and ICs
U101	20821	7805, Regulator
U102	352-27905	7905, Regulator
U103, 105, 106, 107, 108	50313	CA3140, Op-amp
U104	351-10339	LM339, Comparator
Q101	21048	D40D4 NPN Transistor
Q102, 103	30507	2N4124 NPN Transistor
		Zeners and SCRs
D101	50231	LM336, Regulator
D111, 112	35407	IN4742, 12V Zener
TR101	21516	2N5754, Triac
		Diodes
BR101, 102, 103, 104	20111	KBP02, Bridge Rectifiers
D102, 104, 106, 113, 114	21035	1 N914, Diode
D103, 105	15236	1 N4006, Diode
D107, 109	20108	1 N4002, Diode
D110	50286	1 D101, Low Leakage Diodes
		Potentiometers
R140, 141, 147, 151, 153, 154	29119	10K, Trimpot
R181, 182	39532	2.5K, Trimpot

Warranty

ENERGY CONCEPTS, INCORPORATED, warrants this equipment to be free from defective material and workmanship and agrees to remedy any such defect or to furnish a new part in exchange for any part of this unit which under normal installation, use, and service discloses such defect, provided that the unit is delivered by the purchaser to the dealer from whom purchased, or to Energy Concepts, Incorporated, or to a stipulated agent, intact, for the purpose of examination within a period of two years from the date of sale to the original purchases and provided such examination discloses in our judgment that it is defective.

This warranty does not apply if the equipment has been subjected to misuse, neglect, improper installation, used in violation of instructions provided by us, or if repaired or in any way altered outside of our factory or authorized service facility, or if the serial number has been removed, defaced or changed.

Any part approved for remedy or exchange hereunder will be remedied or exchanged without charge to the owner.

Energy Concepts, Inc., assumes no liability for injury, damage, or expense claimed to have been incurred through the use or in the installation of our equipment and products.

This warranty is in lieu all other warranties expressed or implied and no representative or person is authorized to assume for us any other liability in connection with the sale of this equipment.

Further information can be obtained from:

Energy Concepts, Inc.
Chicago, Illinois

Source: Energy Concepts, Inc.

5.3 The Journal Article

Few accomplishments will enhance your professional standing as much as being published. When you publish an article, it tells your professional colleagues not only that you have something original and unique to contribute to your field, but also that it is important enough to be published.

Contrary to popular opinion, the trade journals are always interested in fresh new professional articles. New ideas, new products, new findings, and experiments are the lifeblood of the trade publishing business. It is through the professional and trade journals that the professional, scientific, and academic communities communicate with one another.

The key to a good journal article is its organization and clear purpose. Outlining an article is crucial to its getting published. The subject must be in accordance with the journal's particular subject matter, and your article must have new and interesting information for its readers. Most professional and trade journals have written guidelines for their publishing expectations. Each is unique in its personality and style. Exhibit 5–5 is one example of a good journal article. It demonstrates clear and concise writing techniques found throughout this book.

Exhibit 5–5
Journal Article: "New Booths from Old" (partial)

By JAMES HOWERY, Chief Sales Engineer
Research Products Corporation, Madison, Wisconsin

The paint spray booth is an important element of the finishing operation. If properly engineered and installed and efficiently maintained, the booth provides an efficient and safe working environment for the operators. It does this by drawing particulate and vapors away from the painter. The exhaust also keeps overspray away from products already finished, assuring better finish quality.

Spray booth designs and overspray collection are being closely scrutinized by government regulatory agencies such as OSHA and EPA and city, county, and state regulatory bodies. The selection and installation of a spray booth must be undertaken with the approval of the appropriate agencies.

Changes in chemical coatings and their method of application often result in significant modification of the spray booth and the overspray collection system. Many of the new coating materials are more expensive. The equipment to apply these coatings is more sophisticated. Industry is looking for methods to apply the coatings with maximum transfer efficiency.

Four out of five new booths sold today are equipped with dry filters as the means of collecting overspray. As the industry moves more and more to high-solids coatings, water-borne coatings and powder coatings, while the coating application method puts more of the coating onto the product, the use of dry-filter overspray-collection systems should continue to increase.

There are many dry-filter-booth styles, designs, and configurations, depending on the product being coated. For simplicity, we can reduce the number of booth types to three: totally enclosed; enclosed with conveyor openings; and open-type. Although designs will vary, each booth will comply with the recommendations of the National Fire Protection Association and the Occupational Safety and Health Administration for a minimum of 100 fpm airflow past the spraying operator. This air velocity serves two functions: it draws the solids and vapors away from the operator; and it is sufficient to carry overspray to the overspray collector. There are also

Source: James Howery, "New Booths From Old," *Products Finishing*, May 1985, pp. 66-69. Reprinted with permission.

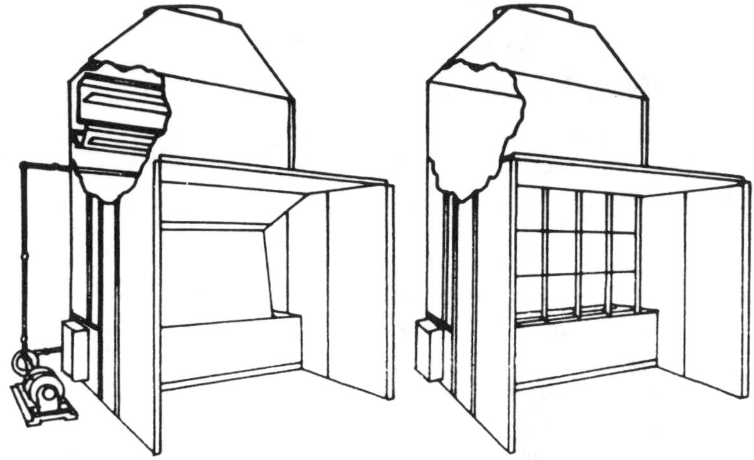

1. WATERWASH SPRAY BOOTH before (left) and after conversion

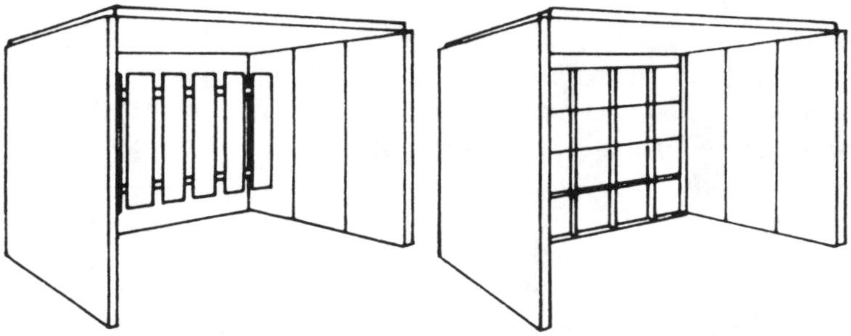

2. BAFFLE-TYPE SPRAY BOOTH before (left) and after conversion

specialty booth designs for electrostatic application that permit as little as 60 fpm air velocity.

All booth manufacturers can provide dry filter overspray collection sections as standard original equipment. Dry filters are adaptable to any style booth design and can be tailored for specific applications.

Conversion. A dry filter exhaust section can be adapted to any existing booth shell, including waterwash booths. It is not unusual to convert an existing booth for as little as $500, thus saving a potential $10,000 investment for a new booth.

The conversion of an old waterwash booth is relatively simple. The two major components of any paint booth are the shell and the exhaust fan. Typically, these can be cleaned up and reused in the converted booth. It is only necessary to incorporate a properly designed overspray collection system in place of the water wash-down sheet, after the plumbing and eliminator plates have been removed, or to put a properly designed collection system in place of the vertically hung baffles. There are literally thousands of older booths in the industry that have been satisfactorily converted.

Figure 1 shows a waterwash booth conversion. Figure 2 shows how a baffle booth can be converted to use dry filters.

High-production spraying operations are incorporating more sophisticated coating-application equipment and procedures that reduce overspray. To further reduce the planned down time, they are now using larger sections of dry filter collectors. The roll form of collector reduces the time required for filter changes, thus increasing productivity. Roll-type media also eliminates the potential of any bypass air and is currently available to meet any of the particulate emission removal requirements.

Appendix

THE MECHANICS OF TECHNICAL WRITING

A.1 The Parts of Speech

Whether you are writing or speaking, you will be using certain basic tools to communicate the message. These basic communication tools are called the *parts of speech.* They are the primary "bricks and mortar" of the English language. There are eight parts of speech, and each of the eight helps to convey a certain type of expressed thought. The eight parts of speech are the following:

1. Nouns
2. Pronouns
3. Verbs
4. Adverbs

5. Adjectives
6. Prepositions
7. Conjunctions
8. Interjections

A.1.1 Nouns

Words that mean persons, places, objects, events, or concepts are called *nouns*. The following words are examples of nouns:

- Persons: technician
  scientist
- Places: factory
  laboratory
- Objects: toggle
  terminal
- Events: explosion
  experiment
- Concepts: formula
  equation

Common, Proper, and Collective Nouns

Nouns are divided into three major classes. Nouns that are common or general people, places, or things are called *common nouns*. Nouns that refer to people, places, or things that are special or particular in and of themselves are called *proper nouns*. (Note: Always capitalize proper nouns.) Nouns thar refer to a single group made up of a number of people, places, or things are called *collective nouns*.

- Common nouns: clinic
  company

- Proper nouns: Mayo Clinic
  Motorola Inc.
- Collective nouns: fleet
  staff

How Nouns Function

Within speech or writing, nouns have certain functions. Nouns can be subjects or objects, and in some cases they can function as adverbs or adjectives. Nouns also have the ability to show possession. The following examples show the basic functions of nouns:

Subject: The *shipment* arrived late that afternoon. [tells who or what is or does something]

Direct object: The receiving inspection department rejected the cold roll *steel*. [tells what was rejected]

Indirect object: Engineering sent him the *specifications*. [tells to whom the specifications were sent]

Object of a preposition: He typed the department code number under the *signature*. [completes the preposition *under*]

Adverb: The tests will be finished *tomorrow*. [tells when the finishing will occur]

Adjective: She is our small *engines* inspector. [tells which one or what kind]

Possession: The HVAC system starts automatically in *Patricia's* area. [shows possession]

Plural Nouns

Most nouns are made plural by simply adding an "s" to the singular form. In some cases, depending on the spelling rule, the noun is pluralized by adding "es" or by changing "y" to "ies." Consider the following examples:

- file — files
- group — groups
- gas — gases
- company — companies

Remember that a collective noun can be singular or plural depending on how it is used.

Singular: The engineering staff meets this morning.

Plural: The engineering staff are still divided about the number of needed tests.

Possessive Nouns

A possessive noun owns or possesses something. You form the possessive by adding " 's" or simply an apostrophe (') to the end of the noun. The possessive noun comes in two forms. They are the singular possessive and the plural possessive.

To form the singular possessive, add " 's" to the noun.

The *company's* trucks are all under warranty.

To form the plural possessive of nouns that end in "s" or "es," simply add an apostrophe to the end of the word.

All the *engineers'* activity reports are due each week.
All of the *secretaries'* wages are above union level.

If the final "s" is a "z" sound, such as in *houses*, add only the apostrophe.

It is necessary to weatherproof the houses' roofs. [the roofs of more than one house]

To form joint ownership or possession, simply make the final noun possessive.

Jack and Pat's project report is due tomorrow.

To form individual ownership or possession of two or more nouns, make each noun possessive.

Jack's and Pat's trip reports are due on Monday.

A.1.2 Pronouns

Pronouns take the place of nouns. Pronouns do virtually everything that nouns do. They create a convenience for the writer by helping to eliminate monotonous repetition of the same noun. The noun that the pronoun replaces is called its *antecedent*. In most cases, replacement of a noun with a pronoun serves to further clarify the noun that is replaced. Pronouns can be divided into seven basic types:

1. Personal pronouns
2. Intensive/reflexive pronouns
3. Indefinite pronouns
4. Possessive pronouns
5. Relative pronouns
6. Interrogative pronouns
7. Demonstrative pronouns

Personal Pronouns

Personal pronouns take the place of a noun that represents a person. They can be and do all the things that a personal noun can do in a sentence.

Subject: *She* is qualified to manage R&D.

Direct object: Show *him* how to set the automatic timers.

Object of preposition: The second shift was managed by *him* for two years.

Possessive: We want to have *your* findings by Thursday morning.

Intensive: The manager *herself* rejected the shipment.

Reflexive: I basically taught *myself* the order-entry system.

The following table shows all the forms or cases for personal pronouns in the first, second, and third person.

Person	**Case**	**Singular**	**Plural**
First:	nominative	I	we
	possessive	my/mine	our/ours
	objective	me	us
	intensive/ reflexive	myself	ourselves
Second:	nominative	you	you
	possessive	your/yours	your/yours
	objective	you	you
	intensive/ reflexive	yourself	yourselves
Third:	nominative	he/she/it	they
	possessive	his/her, hers/ its	their/theirs
	objective	him/her/it	them
	intensive/ reflexive	himself/ herself/ itself	themselves

(Baugh, *Essentials of English Grammar*. National Textbook Company, 1993.)

Indefinite Pronouns

Indefinite pronouns show unspecified people or things. Many of the indefinite pronouns will show quantity, such as *all, several, none, few*. The most common indefinite pronouns are the following:

all	each	most	other
another	either	neither	several
any	everybody	nobody	some
anybody	everyone	none	somebody

anyone	few	no one	someone
both	many	one	such

(Baugh, *Essentials of English Grammar.* National Textbook Company, 1993.)

Consider the following examples of indefinite pronouns:

The plastics department appointed a new group leader for the day shift. They appointed *someone* from outside of the section. [*Someone* replaces *group leader* from the preceding sentence.]

Do you have the newest edition of the operations manuals? We have *none* in our section. [*None* replaces *manuals.*]

Possessive Pronouns

Possessive pronouns do all the things that possessive nouns do. The major difference is that possessive pronouns never take an apostrophe. Consider the following examples:

Whose caliper was left on the bench? [*Who* is never possessive, but *whose* is possessive.]

I thought *my* tools were lost. *Mine* were found the next day.

Our test project starts on Monday. Those parking spaces on the north end of the lot are *ours*.

How did *your* figures come out? Are these figures *yours*?

His/her timing on this matter was perfect. *Hers* was the best.

Do these tools belong in our department or *theirs*? *Their* department is also in the pool.

A problem frequently occurs with the contraction *it's* and the possessive *its*. Remember the common rule: possessive pronouns do not take an apostrophe.

It's crucial to run the machine according to *its* operations manual.

Relative Pronouns

Relative pronouns are primarily used to keep from repeating the same noun within one or several closely linked sentences. The relative pronouns *who, whom, whose,* and *that* typically refer to people. The pronouns *which*, *that*, and *of which* refer to things.

> The new Brinnel hardness tester, *which* she purchased recently, is a valuable tool.
>
> The employee *who* discarded the scrap brass has been reprimanded.

Interrogative Pronouns

Interrogative pronouns always ask a question. The pronouns *who, whose,* and *whom* all refer to people. The pronouns *what* and *which* refer to objects or concepts.

> *Who* shut down the line?
> *What* is your highest estimate of damage?
> *Which* vehicle should we take?

Demonstrative Pronouns

Demonstrative pronouns do two things. They first indicate a specific item or group of items as antecedent. The second thing they do is show distance from the speaker or writer.

> *This* is our work area, and *that* is our lunchroom. [The work area is closer to the speaker than is the lunchroom.]
>
> I don't envy *those* involved in the layoff this fall. [*Those* has no specific antecedent; it refers to a specific group that was involved in a layoff.]

Pronoun-Antecedent Agreement

Antecedents are the nouns to which pronouns refer. Pronouns must agree with their antecedent. This means that the number, case, and person of the pronoun must be the same as the noun to which it refers.

> Software engineers must have a working knowledge of FORTRAN. Otherwise, they will have problems devising routines. [The antecedent is *engineers*. It agrees with its pronoun, *they*, in number.]

Who and *whom* seem to present problems to many writers. The difficulty is a matter of when to use either of the forms. Simply use *who* as a subject and use *whom* as an object.

A.1.3 Verbs

Verbs express three primary things to the reader. They show a sense of being, a sense of action, and a sense of time. Because of these three elements, verbs form the core of expressive writing.

The State of Being Verb

Verbs that express being or condition are also called *linking verbs*. This is because they link or connect the subject of the sentence with a noun, pronoun, or adjective that describes the subject.

That element *is* inert.
She *is* the leading chemist in the field.
We *are* not an engineering group.

The most common state of being verb is the verb *to be*. Other common linking verbs are the following:

- appear
- become
- feel
- grow
- look
- hear
- seem
- sound
- remain

State of being verbs also function as auxiliary verbs or "helping verbs." These verbs "help" certain verb constructions to express themselves as a complete verb form. They can signal a change in tense or a change in voice. Consider the following:

The lab *has tested* for carbon.
R&D *is testing* for carbon content.
She *can operate* the CNC lathe.

Active and Passive Voice

Verbs can show only one other state besides being, and that state is action. They show that something is happening. To show action in a sentence, you can express it either actively or passively. The active or passive way of expressing that action in the sentence is called *voice*. The *active voice* expresses action in an active manner, while the *passive voice* expresses the action passively.

> ***Active voice:*** Everyone in the engineering department must write a weekly activity report. [The subject of the sentence (everyone) acts directly (must write) on a direct object (report).]
>
> ***Passive voice:*** An activity report must be written by everyone in the engineering department. [The subject of the sentence is what is acted on (report).]

The passive verb form is made up of the auxiliary verb *to be* "helping" the past participle *written*. The actor in this sentence (everyone) has been made the object of the preposition *by*. As a technical writer, you should prefer the active voice, because it is more direct and lively for your reader.

Verbals

Verbals are derived from verbs. They are verb forms that act as other grammatical elements, such as nouns, adverbs, and adjectives, within a sentence. There are three types of verbals:

- Infinitives
- Participles
- Gerunds

Infinitives An infinitive is a verbal. It is the root form of a verb without the restriction imposed through number, tense, and person. Infinitives are generally preceded by the word *to*. Infinitives can be used within a sentence as nouns, adverbs, and adjectives.

He likes *to experiment*. [noun]

It is the last partition *to build*. [adjective]

The solenoid acts *to stop* the flow of liquid. [adverb]

Participles A verb that is used as an adjective is called a *participle*. There are both past participles and present participles. Most present participles end in "ing," and most past participles end in "ed," "en," "ed," or "t."

The *finished* version of the report was not handed out.

Past participles are used with a linking form of the verb *to be* in order to form the passive voice verb form.

The specifications were *written* by the new engineer.

Gerunds The gerund is a verbal that is used as a noun. Gerunds always end in "ing" and signal the use of an action verb to be used as a noun.

Testing is a major activity in the R&D lab.

Verb Tenses

Verb tenses deal with time. In any sentence, the time element will always be expressed by the verb. That state of time expressed by the verb is called *tense*.

In English, verbs have six regular tenses and two special function tenses.

Regular tenses:

- Present
- Past
- Future
- Present perfect
- Past perfect
- Future perfect

Special functions:

- Progressive
- Conditional

Present Tense The present tense expresses an action or a state of being that is occurring at the present time. The present tense also indicates habitual action or something that is true at all times. The present tense is best used with technical definitions, descriptions, and instructions.

I write technical specifications.

Past Tense The past tense expresses action or being that occurred in the past and is not continuing into the present.

I wrote the specifications yesterday.

Future Tense The future tense expresses an action or state of being that will occur in the future.

I will write the specifications tomorrow.

Perfect Tenses The perfect tenses express actions and states of being that happen at one time but are understood in relation to another time. They signify totally completed actions. The perfect tenses are found in the present, past, and future tense verb constructions.

I have written the report. [present perfect]

I had written the report. [past perfect]

I will have written the report. [future perfect]

The Progressive Verb Form The progressive verb form indicates action and being that are continuous relative to the tense.

I am writing the report. [present progressive]

I was writing the report. [past progressive]

I will be writing the report. [future progressive]

The Conditional Verb Form The conditional verb form expresses the intent or possibility to do or be something.

I can write the report. [present conditional]

I could have written the report. [past conditional]

Consider the following full conjugation of the verb *to write*:

Present:
I write
you write
he/she/it writes
we write
you write
they write

am/is/are writing [progressive]
can/could write [conditional]

Past:
I wrote
you wrote
he/she/it wrote
we wrote
you wrote
they wrote

was/were writing [past progressive]
could write/could have written/ could have been writing [past conditional]

Future:
I will/shall write
you will/shall write
he/she/it will/shall write
we will/shall write
you will/shall write
they will/shall write

will/shall be writing [future progressive]

Present perfect:
I have written
you have written
he/she/it has written
we have written
you have written
they have written
have been/has been writing

Past perfect:
I had written
you had written
he/she/it had written
we had written
you had written
they had written

had been writing

Future perfect:
I will have written
you will have written
he/she/it will have written
we will have written
you will have written
they will have written

will have been writing

Mood

Verbs express differences in the speaker's or writer's intention. The sense of intention is called *mood*. There are three moods in English:

1. The *indicative mood* makes a direct statement or asks a question.
   The train is ten minutes late.
   Is the train running late?
2. The imperative mood commands, directs, or requests.
   Call the warehouse and cancel the shipment.

3. The *subjunctive mood* makes a statement of urgency, formality, possibility, or speculation.

   She demanded that they check it immediately.
   They recommended that the testing procedure be adopted.
   If she were to sign the release, she would have no legal recourse later.
   If he were the director, policies would change.

Subject-Verb Agreement

Verbs are like pronouns in that verbs must agree with their subjects in person and number.

Agreement in person:
I am
You are
It is

Agreement in number:
She writes
They write

A.1.4 Adjectives

Adjectives modify, describe, and explain nouns, pronouns, and other adjectives. Adjectives answer the questions of *what kind? how many? which one?* and *how much?*

The *feasibility* report was due yesterday. [what kind]

There are more than *forty* failures per year. [how many]

She tested *those* o-rings this morning. [which one]

We tested the *larger* sample. [how much]

Adjectives can be divided into five general types

- Demonstrative
- Limiting

- Comparative
- Compound
- Predicate

Demonstrative Adjectives

Demonstrative adjectives show or demonstrate particular items and their distance from the speaker. Typical demonstrative adjectives are *this, that, which, what, these, those.*

> *This* sampling shows a definite skew toward *that* sampling. [*This* is closer to the speaker than *that.*]

Limiting Adjectives

Limiting adjectives identify and number the nouns they modify. In most cases, the limiting adjective comes before the noun it modifies. Typical limiting adjectives are:

- a/an
- the
- few
- many
- every
- each
- every
- both
- several
- some
- any
- most
- one

> *Few* engines will pass those tests.

Comparative Adjectives

Many adjectives make comparisons of people, places, and things. The positive, comparative, and superlative adjectives show different degrees of the quality or characteristic. The following examples are some typical comparative adjectives:

Positive:	***Comparative:***	***Superlative:***
hard	hard	hardest
careful	more careful	most careful
large	larger	largest
small	smaller	smallest
good	better	best

Compound Adjectives

Compound adjectives are hyphenated forms when they precede the noun they modify. If they follow the noun they modify, they are two separate words.

This is a *past-due* report.
This report is past due.

Predicate Adjectives

Adjectives following linking verbs are called *predicate adjectives.* They refer to and modify the condition of the subject and its relation to the verb.

The lubricant has become hot.

A.1.5 Adverbs

Adverbs describe and explain verbs. They clarify questions about verbs, such as *when? where? how much?* and *how?* Adverbs explain an action verb or state of being verb in expanded detail and provide a more vivid picture of that verb.

Most adverbs end in "ly" and come from nouns and adjectives. In some cases both the adjective and adverb will end in "ly."

Noun:	***Adjective:***	***Adverb:***
care	careful	carefully
hour	hourly	hourly

Adverbs showing when:

now	forever	frequently
before	seldom	often
once	Friday	eventually
never	occasionally	always

Adverbs showing where:

in	through	across
over	under	sideways
upstairs	here	backwards
out	there	around

Adverbs showing how much:

entirely	thoroughly	excessively
mostly	nearly	mildly
completely		

Adverbs showing how:

nicely	quickly	tirelessly
carefully	equally	accurately
orderly		

A.1.6 Prepositions

Prepositions are the words that connect informational phrases to the rest of a sentence. A prepositional phrase always expands and adds meaningful information. Prepositions have objects, which together form the prepositional phrase. Prepositional phrases can serve as adjectives and adverbs.

> Signal strength is still *within range of the original cell site.* [*Within range* modifies the verb *is*. The phrase *of the original cell site* modifies the noun *strength*.]

The following is a list of some commonly used prepositions:

above	below	of
across	between	off
after	beyond	on
against	by	over

along	down	through
around	for	to
at	from	under
before	in	up
behind	like	with

A.1.7 Conjunctions

Conjunctions connect major elements within sentences and show their relationships. There are four basic types of conjunction:

- coordinating conjunction
- correlative conjunction
- subordinating conjunction
- linking adverb

Coordinating Conjunctions

Coordinating conjunctions join two or more elements in a sentence. The elements joined together can be nouns, verbs, adjectives, adverbs, pronouns, or phrases and clauses. The coordinating conjunctions are *and, but, or,* and *nor.*

The *spindle and centers* were faulty on the lathe.

Correlative Conjunctions

Correlative conjunctions are used in pairs to emphasize the elements they join. The elements that they join are of equal importance. The following are some typical correlative conjunctions:

- either— or
- neither— nor
- not only—but also
- both— and

The chemical analysis performed on the last batch was *neither* complete *nor* accurate.

Subordinating Conjunctions

Subordinating conjunctions also emphasize the elements they join, but, unlike correlative conjunctions, subordinating conjunctions join elements of unequal importance or rank. These elements are generally subordinate clauses and independent clauses. The following are some common subordinating conjunctions:

after	provided	what
although	since	when
as	than	where
because	that	which
before	though	while
how	unless	who
if	until	

Subordinating conjunctions introduce sentences as well as join elements within them. Subordinating conjunctions at the beginning of subordinating clauses at the beginning of sentences are always followed by a comma. No comma is needed when the subordinate clause comes at the end of the sentence.

We should keep these data in the current data bank *until* new tests are completed.

Until new tests are completed, we must keep these data in the current data bank.

Many clauses give additional information about a person, place, or thing. When that clause is essential to the meaning of the sentence, it is known as a *restrictive clause*. When the clause is descriptive but not essential, it is called a *nonrestrictive clause*.

The lab *where the fire started* was a total loss. [restrictive clause]

The other compressor, *which was never used,* was not damaged in the move. [nonrestrictive clause]

Linking Adverbs

Linking adverbs join two independent clauses. They indicate the relationship between two ideas expressed in independent clauses. As a general rule, linking adverbs show results, contrast, or continuation.

Linking adverbs can follow a semicolon at the beginning of the second clause they are joining. They can also be within the second clause, set off with commas.

> Further tests delayed shipment; *therefore*, the project was put on temporary hold.
>
> Further tests delayed shipment; the project, therefore, was put on hold.

A.1.8 Interjections

Interjections express emotion or get the reader's immediate attention. In technical writing, you should not use interjections to express emotion—this is primarily used as a literary device. You can, however, use interjections effectively as attention getters where your reader should pay special attention, such as when safety is an issue.

> *Beware!* Poisonous fumes are released in this chemical reaction.
>
> *Warning!* High voltage.

A.2 Punctuation

Punctuation is unique to written language. You don't use punctuation when you speak. What you do use is a series of meaningful pauses and tonal changes in the sound of your voice. Because there is no sound in written language, a great deal of meaning is lost unless some kind of substitute for these vocal pauses and intonations is used.

Consequently, a series of coded marks have been created in written language to accommodate this need. These marks are punctuation marks that let the reader know when there are such things as pauses and voice modulation that signal added meaning.

The following are the primary punctuation marks of written English:

- Period [.]
- Question mark [?]
- Exclamation mark [!]
- Comma [,]
- Semicolon [;]
- Colon [:]
- Hyphen [-]
- Dash [–]
- Brackets [ ]
- Parentheses [( )]
- Ellipses [. . .]

A.2.1 Period

Periods end sentences. They signal a pause that is sufficiently long to be termed a stop. Periods are only used to end declarative and imperative sentences.

That tank will hold only 40 gallons of the fuel. [declarative]
Please submit all activity reports on the Monday following the week's activity. [imperative]

Periods are also used to abbreviate various words and titles.

- free on board — F.O.B.
- Department of Defense — D.O.D.

- President — Pres.
- Captain — Capt.

A.2.2 Question Mark

Question marks end questions or interrogative sentences.

Were all the instruments packed in protective materials?

A.2.3 Exclamation Mark

An exclamation mark forces emphatic attention to a statement. It is like shouting with the writing. In technical writing, these marks can be effective in drawing attention to warnings and special attention notes.

- Beware!
- Do not use near open flame!

A.2.4 Comma

Commas are the great plague of most writers. No one seems sure of just when and when not to use them. There are many established rules about when to use a comma, and we will cite a few. But principles, rather than memorized rules, are the easiest guidelines for comma use. There are two great guiding principles for using commas:

1. Use a comma when it helps clarify technical information for your reader.
2. Use a comma where you would make a definite and natural pause if you were speaking.

These general principles are especially evident in the case of items in a series and introductory elements in sentences.

Commas separate items in a series. They do this so the items don't get jumbled and blurred together in the sentence.

> Each kit should contain a *Brinnel hardness tester, micrometer, calipers, and a steel machinist's rule*.

Introductory subordinate clauses, phrases, and expressions should be set off with commas. All of these openers force a natural pause for clarity.

> *When the R&D facility was opened last year,* some of the engineering staff had no individual work areas.

Commas always set off nonrestrictive clauses. These serve as additional informational material within the sentence.

> The seminar on superconductors, *held in October*, had high attendance from our section.

A.2.5 Semicolon

From a literary standpoint, a semicolon indicates a strong pause, but not a strong enough pause for a period. From a technical writing standpoint, use the period. Whereas it is true that semicolons separate two independent clauses, it makes for much more simplified and easily read technical prose to make two sentences of the two independent clauses.

Semicolons are also used to separate items in a series. In technical prose it is far more effective to set off the list after a full colon rather than to separate items in the text with a semicolon.

A.2.6 Colon

Like a semicolon, a colon indicates a strong pause, but not a strong enough pause for a period. A colon has great use to the technical writer in setting off lists of items. Setting off a list with a colon is by far the most effective way to use lists.

Bring the following items to the presentation:
Two projectors
Slides
Flip chart
Screen
Lectern

A.2.7 Quotation Marks

Quotation marks signal your reader that you are quoting the exact words of someone else.

Her exact words were "The first test results show only marginal success."

Quotation marks also enclose the titles of certain publications:

- Articles
- Book chapters
- Reports
- Government publications
- Conference/seminar titles
- Proceedings

The ASTD titled this year's international conference "The Year of the Technician."
(Titles of books and periodicals are underlined, to be typeset in italics.)

A.2.8 Apostrophe

Apostrophes show possession and signal contractions.

Bring the manual to the *technician's* work area. [possession]
The new procedure *didn't* work out well. [contraction]

Indefinite pronouns use an apostrophe to show possession.

someone's wrench
everybody's responsibility
no one's fault

Personal pronouns do not use an apostrophe for possession.

her report
his truck
your tests

A.2.9 Hyphen

Hyphens join as well as divide key elements in a sentence. The following examples show how hyphens are used in technical writing.

Hyphens:

- Join words used as a single unit in a sentence:

The *decision-making* process will take place at all levels.

- Join numbers:

thirty-seven-year-old manufacturing plant
two-thirds full

- Indicate continuous numbers:

pages 54-68 of the report

- Join compound adjectives:

decision-making process
well-run facility

(Note: If one of the modifiers is an adverb ending in "ly" or if the modifier follows the noun, no hyphen is used.)

publicly owned power plant
the process of decision making

A.2.10 Dash

Dashes show a break in thought or additional information within the context of the sentence. A dash is formed in type using two hyphens. Do not put spaces before or after the dash.

> This overhead tram--not the one in Warehouse 2--needs routine maintenance performed on the cables.

A.2.11 Parentheses

Parentheses enclose a break in thought or additional information within the context of the sentence.

> The new lab (at our Oregon facility) will house the new testing equipment.

A.3 Sentence Structure

A.3.1 Complete Sentences

Sentences are complete thoughts put into words (whether written or spoken). In order to be a complete thought, each sentence must have two primary ingredients: a subject and a verb. If either or both of these two things are missing, it is not a sentence.

Sentences convey four basic types of thought:

1. Declarative
2. Interrogative
3. Imperative
4. Exclamatory

Declarative

A declarative sentence makes a statement of fact. It declares information.

Cellular communication is made up of radio signals.

Interrogative

An interrogative sentence asks a question.

Where is the nearest cell site?

Imperative

An imperative sentence gives a command. It tells the reader to do something.

Put on your protective eyewear.

Exclamatory

An exclamatory sentence gives extreme emphasis to the statement. It tends to "shout" at the reader. Exclamatory sentences are primarily literary devices and are not used frequently in technical writing. Exclamatory sentences do have use in such things as "warning" sentences.

Danger! Use extreme caution when handling!

A.3.2 Sentence Fragments

A sentence fragment is a partial thought that is missing either the subject, the verb, or both. Without either of these two ingredients, the sentence is incomplete and is called a *sentence fragment*. Both of the following are fragments:

Decided by the safety committee for the handbook. [no subject]

Safety rules by the safety committee for the handbook. [no verb]

A.3.3 Run-On Sentences

A run-on sentence is two or more complete thoughts without clarifying punctuation in one sentence.

Our department cannot perform the tests on your materials because of missing parts in your sampling kits and we tried to notify you of this problem earlier in the week. [run-on]

Our department cannot perform the tests on your materials because of missing parts in your sampling kits. We tried to notify you of this problem earlier in the week. [This revision simply made the run-on into two simple declarative sentences.]

A.3.4 Phrases

A phrase is a group of related words without a subject or verb. There are four types of phrases:

1. Prepositional phrase
   on the edge
   from different tests

2. Verb phrase
   has been said
   was told

3. Participial phrase
   writing the report
   tested for tensile strength

4. Infinitive phrase
   to test
   to combine

A.3.5 Clauses

Clauses are groups of words that contain a subject and verb. There are two types of clauses. *Independent clauses* can stand alone and therefore qualify as a complete sentence. *Subordinate clauses* also have a subject and verb, but they convey a thought that is dependent on another element or clause to be complete as a thought.

> ***Independent clause:*** The testing procedures have changed, but the technicians didn't realize it. [This clause qualifies as a complete sentence.]
> ***Subordinate clause:*** Since the testing procedures have changed, the technicians read the new manual. [This subordinate clause needs more information to be complete. The word *since* causes the clause to become subordinate.]

A.3.6 Sentence Types

There are four basic types of sentences in terms of their mechanical clause structure:

- Simple sentence
- Compound sentence
- Complex sentence
- Compound-complex sentence

Simple Sentence

A simple sentence is an independent clause without subordinate clauses or other independent clauses. It is the basic subject/verb statement.

> The new manager started yesterday.

Compound Sentence

A compound sentence is two or more independent clauses without any subordinate clauses.

> We have one week to finish the analysis, or we will have to postpone the project indefinitely.

Complex Sentence

A complex sentence is an independent clause and one or more subordinate clauses.

> After she read the report, she took immediate action.

Compound-Complex Sentence

Even though we don't really need one more week to finish the tests, the project will be postponed, and it will be given the extra testing time.

INDEX

About the Author

James Shelton is president of Shelton and Associates, a Chicago-based communications consulting firm providing training programs in technical writing, business writing, and marketing to client firms that include Motorola, Inc., Baxter Healthcare Corp., and Beverly Banks, Inc. James Shelton also is an adjunct professor in the Graduate School of Communications at Roosevelt University, Chicago, and teaches technical writing at Elgin Community College, Elgin, Illinois.

TITLES OF INTEREST IN BUSINESS AND INTERNATIONAL BUSINESS